Understanding Applied Learning

Understanding Applied Learning enables teachers, lecturers and educators to facilitate applied learning effectively with learners in schools, colleges and universities. It introduces teachers to the concept of applied learning in practice, cutting across any vocational and academic divide to show how this approach supports high-quality and effective outcomes for learners. Applied learning prepares and equips learners for life in the twenty-first century and lifelong learning. Offering practical guidance on why and how to adopt applied learning in all post-primary settings, this practical resource introduces and explores the core concepts, practices and benefits of using this approach. Illustrated with real-life scenarios, it examines why applied learning is relevant today, how it enables learners to connect knowledge with new situations, how to navigate and solve intellectual and skills-based problems and how to work collaboratively and develop higher-level thinking skills.

Key topics covered include:

- A range of applied learning theories and strategies
- Relevant, Engaging, Active Learning (REAL) for successful knowledge and skills development
- The relevance of applied learning to employers
- Overcoming issues in embedding applied learning approaches
- How to embed creativity into learning experiences.

Understanding Applied Learning is an authoritative, down-to-earth guide to facilitate applied learning effectively and successfully with students in secondary schools, colleges and universities. It is a source of support and inspiration for all those committed to high-quality and effective outcomes for learners.

Dr Tanya Ovenden-Hope is a committed and enthusiastic educationalist with nearly 30 years' experience in teaching, teacher education and educational leadership. An innovative academic, Tanya has maintained scholarly engagement in educational improvement and effectiveness throughout her career. Her commitment to championing the importance of, and developing new ways of thinking about, learning and teaching was recognised when she was awarded Principal Fellow of the Higher Education Academy in 2015 and the National Enterprise Educator Award in 2014.

Tanya began her career as a Sociology 'A' Level Lecturer in a Further Education (FE) college. She continued to teach and lead Sociology for 10 years, in FE and secondary education. While working as Head of Sociology and Head of Year 12 in a school, Tanya co-authored her first book, *Sociology in Perspective*. She also began to use research to develop her understanding of how to enhance and improve learning opportunities. This led to Tanya not only writing more books for Sociology students and teachers, but also achieving an MA in Education and working as a guest lecturer for University Education courses.

Realising a desire to develop teaching to improve learning, Tanya has focused on Education for the last 15 years with roles developing and leading teacher education, and teaching and learning, in FE and Higher Education. She has maintained her academic engagement, achieving a Doctorate in Education in 2004 (while working full time) and has honorary roles that include Visiting Research Fellow at Plymouth University and adjunct Professor in Education at Cape Breton University. An active member of the educational community at all levels, Tanya is also a school governor and Director; Executive Council member of the Universities Council for the Education of Teachers (UCET) and Special Interest Group (SIG) Convenor for the British Educational Research Association (BERA). Tanya is currently Director of Educational Research and Development with The Cornwall College Group, a very large group of colleges located in the South West of England, and leads Learning, Teaching and

Assessment, Educational curriculum and externally funded educational intervention research.

Tanya is author of over 75 papers, reports, articles and books written for learners, teachers, leaders, academics and policy makers.

Professor Sonia Blandford is one of the country's foremost experts on improving the education and aspirations of children from disadvantaged backgrounds. She focuses on providing the leadership in schools to create equal chances for all. Sonia was named in Debrett's 2016 list of the Top 500 Most Influential People in the UK, and is among the 2016 Women of the Year. She is Chair of the Blackpool Challenge and also a Founding Trustee of the College of Teaching.

Sonia has been a music teacher since 1980, working in primary and secondary schools across England. She is currently founder and CEO of the award-winning educational charity Achievement for All, which provides programmes to improve outcomes for children and young people aged 2 to 19 years, vulnerable to underachievement, in 4,000 early-years, school and post-16 settings in England and Wales; and professor of education and social enterprise at UCL Institute of Education.

Previously, Sonia was director of research and leadership at Teach First; professor of educational leadership and innovation at the University of Warwick, where she now holds an honorary professorship; pro-vice chancellor and dean of education at Canterbury Christ Church University; deputy dean of the Westminster Institute of Education, Oxford Brookes University and honorary senior research Fellow at the University of Oxford. Prior to her charity and higher education positions, Sonia has also held leadership positions in five secondary schools in Wiltshire, Bath, London and Bristol.

As an innovator in education Sonia led the creation and development of the Teach First initial teacher training programme and EdD programmes at Oxford Brookes University and Canterbury Christ Church University, each aiming to provide the highest quality professional development opportunities for teachers. Sonia was among the first cohort to be awarded an EdD in the UK at the University of Bristol (1995). She was a member of the inaugural NPQH development and delivery team in the South West and has been a quality assurance assessor monitoring quality and standards in higher education. Sonia is currently a leading researcher in the European Agency OECD Raising Attainment project.

In a voluntary capacity, Sonia has founded and supported seven local and national charities that share her commitment to enabling every child to achieve regardless of background, challenge or need. Her first charity, The Corsham Windband Association, has engaged children and young people from diverse backgrounds in music making for over 30 years.

Sonia is author of 150 articles and books written for teachers, leaders, parents and carers, and children and young people, most recently publishing with John Catt and Bloomsbury.

Understanding Applied Learning

Developing Effective Practice to Support All Learners

**Tanya Ovenden-Hope
and Sonia Blandford**

LONDON AND NEW YORK

First published 2018
by Routledge
2 Park Square, Milton Park, Abingdon, Oxon OX14 4RN

and by Routledge
711 Third Avenue, New York, NY 10017

Routledge is an imprint of the Taylor & Francis Group, an informa business

© 2018 Tanya Ovenden-Hope and Sonia Blandford

The right of Tanya Ovenden-Hope and Sonia Blandford to be identified as the authors of this work has been asserted by them in accordance with sections 77 and 78 of the Copyright, Designs and Patents Act 1988.

All rights reserved. No part of this book may be reprinted or reproduced or utilised in any form or by any electronic, mechanical, or other means, now known or hereafter invented, including photocopying and recording, or in any information storage or retrieval system, without permission in writing from the publishers.

Trademark notice: Product or corporate names may be trademarks or registered trademarks, and are used only for identification and explanation without intent to infringe.

British Library Cataloguing in Publication Data
A catalogue record for this book is available from the British Library

Library of Congress Cataloging in Publication Data
A catalog record for this book has been requested

ISBN: 978-1-138-91120-8 (hbk)
ISBN: 978-1-138-91121-5 (pbk)
ISBN: 978-1-315-69290-6 (ebk)

Typeset in Celeste and Optima
by Florence Production Ltd, Stoodleigh, Devon, UK

 Printed in the United Kingdom by Henry Ling Limited

Contents

List of figures and tables	xi
Acknowledgements	xiii
Introduction	1
1 What is applied learning?	9
Defining applied learning	11
Experiential learning	12
Active learning	13
Applied learning	13
Applied learning and the practice of teachers	14
Inquiry-based teaching and learning	15
Assessment	17
Collaborative learning	19
Technology	20
Collaboration with colleagues	23
Systems for teachers	24
Summary	25
2 The theory and 'pedagogy' of applied learning	29
Personalised learning	30
Independent learning and metacognition	31
The challenge of applied learning	32
Why are teenagogy and applied learning so important?	33

vii

Contents

	Using applied learning approaches to meet the challenges of teenagogy	38
	Removing barriers to participation, learning and achievement	38
	Stretching and challenging learners	40
	Meeting learners' individual needs	41
	Creating independent learners	43
	Summary	44
3	**Applied learning in teaching**	**47**
	What applied learning means in practice	48
	Applied learning and teaching strategies	55
	Summary	59
4	**Applied learning, employment and employers**	**61**
	Applied learning and skills for employment	61
	Applied learning: Aspects of teaching practice for employer engagement	62
	Mentoring	63
	Team-working and team-building	65
	Building the team	67
	Motivating teams	70
	Applied learning: Areas for developing learners' skills for employment	71
	Work-related learning on non-vocational courses	71
	Work-related learning on vocational courses	75
	Employer engagement	76
	Summary	80
5	**Facilitating applied learning**	**83**
	The role of the teacher: What does a teacher *do* to facilitate applied learning?	84
	Inclusive practice	86
	The teacher–learner relationship and applied learning	91
	Increasing aspiration and access: The route to higher achievement	93

viii

Contents

Learner mindset	94
Collaborative learning	96
Problem-based learning	97
Functional skills	100
What are functional skills?	100
How should we teach functional skills?	101
Health and safety for applied learning	103
Summary	104

6 Creativity in applied learning — 107

Why is creativity important?	107
Creativity in applied learning	110
The creative teacher as researcher	114
Action research	115
Summary	117

7 Reflective learning and self-evaluation in practice — 119

Reflective learning	120
Self-evaluation	121
A model for self-evaluation	124
Monitoring	126
Evaluation	127
Summary	129

Conclusion	131
Glossary	133
Index	137

Figures and tables

Figures

1.1	The applied learning cycle	12
4.1	Tuckman's (1965) stages of team-building	69
7.1	A model for self-evaluation	125

Tables

2.1	Pedagogy, andragogy and teenagogy	34
3.1	Applied learning strategies	57
7.1	Self-evaluation situations	123

Acknowledgements

Our thanks go to:

Stefan Burkey for acting as technical consultant (and epic support) for the final stages of this work;

Sally Griffin and Liz McKenzie for their ideas and contributions early on in the process when this was going to be a different book;

Sandie Johns and Rory Mason for providing great case studies (and for being advocates of applied learning in their practice);

Patric Ovenden-Hope for helping with last minute jpeg issues when all other routes and sources failed.

Introduction

Imagine that you are at home on an early afternoon in the winter. The temperature is barely in positive numbers; snow is forecast for this evening . . . and your heating and hot water has stopped working.

A gas engineer – Harriet – has arrived at your home and has examined your gas-fired boiler. Harriet explains that she is going to have to replace a section of the pipe that carries the gas inside your boiler. To do this, Harriet will have to cut the pipe apart.

Harriet reassures you that she has studied every piece of legislation relating to health and safety, has read every industry 'best practice' guide on how to prevent carbon monoxide poisoning and gas explosions, and has spent all morning reading the technical specifications and schematics of your boiler. However, Harriet has neglected to mention that she has never picked up a spanner or a hacksaw before and has never actually looked inside a boiler.

This scenario would not occur in real life. A registered gas engineer will have been trained in both the theoretical knowledge *and* the practice-based skills needed to diagnose technical problems and how to solve them in a safe and effective way.

1

Introduction

This praxis-based approach to learning, bringing together both theory and practice, is used in a wide range of professions for initial training, education and continuing professional development. In fact, it is difficult to find a profession that uses any form of 'hands-on' practice – from architecture to zoology – that does not use this approach to learning in some way.

The focus of this book is on how to facilitate applied learning effectively with learners in post-primary settings (although some of the ideas will work well for these younger learners too). We want to introduce teachers to the concept of applied learning in practice, cutting across any vocational and academic divide to show how this approach supports high quality and effective outcomes for learners. Applied learning prepares and equips learners for life in twenty-first century and lifelong learning. We do not offer a historical overview or theoretical critique of applied learning, but provide some practical considerations for why and how to adopt it in a classroom, workplace learning setting or educational institution.

A good starting point to understanding applied learning is to draw on an example of a theory- and practice-based education, which can be found in the medical profession. Medical students study a range of knowledge bases, theories and concepts that they then apply to practice using models, cadavers and live patients. They go on to assist experienced surgeons, first taking part in simple operations and diagnoses and then undertaking increasingly complex surgeries and cases as their skills and (successful) independence develops.

Medical training is a great example of applied learning. Applied learning does what it says on the tin; it is based on, and applied to, real-life scenarios relevant to what is being learned. Applied learning equips learners to navigate and solve intellectual and skills-based problems, to apply that learning to new situations, and to develop higher-level thinking skills.

Applied learning can incorporate a variety of learning strategies, but most commonly is linked to and can incorporate Problem-Based Learning (PBL). The medical approach to training

Introduction

typically adopts PBL when applying learning. Stanford University defines PBL as '[a] Curriculum development and delivery system that recognizes the need to develop problem solving skills as well as the necessity of helping students to acquire necessary knowledge and skills' (Stanford University, n.d.).

When training to become a doctor, medical students will use applied learning when developing their skills of diagnoses, engaging with PBL to solve and create treatment plans for case study patient illnesses. A case study patient will present with symptoms that require the learner to research the problem, and identify relevant sources of information that could explain why the patient is ill and how they could be treated. The learners will have some existing knowledge, they will know where to source further information and will work together to find solutions that form a diagnosis and suggested treatment. Note that PBL works well when learners work together, as it enables them to share knowledge, skills and ideas to solve the problem more effectively (we provide more information on applied learning in teaching in Chapter 3).

While this approach to learning appears more commonplace in higher education, we argue that applied learning can (and does) provide rich and meaningful opportunities for learners in many age ranges in schools, colleges and universities (Chapter 2 addresses issues of pedagogy, with a special focus on facilitating applied learning with 14–19-year-old learners). We also suggest that there is a growing body of research which suggests that applied learning is an ideal vehicle for equipping young people today with the skills and capacities that they will need to fully engage with their working and wider lives in the twenty-first century, and possibly even the twenty-second century (Chapter 4 explores applied learning and skills for employment).

If we consider the educational landscape today, a significant number of curriculum expectations, at all levels and across vocational and academic disciplines, place an increasing emphasis on *applying learning* in different contexts, across

3

Introduction

varying topics and beyond subject boundaries. In this book we identify case studies of applied learning within the curriculum to support your understanding of how this works in practice.

The roots of applied learning

Applied learning as an approach to the teaching and learning of children and young people has a, perhaps surprisingly, long history.

It is possible to argue that the origins of applied learning can be seen in the work of Fröbel (1826) and the ethos and approach of the nineteenth-century kindergarten movement in the USA.

In 1897, John Dewey stated that his landmark pedagogical approach was based on a belief that:

> the school must represent present life – life as real and vital to the child as that which he carries on in the home, in the neighborhood, or on the playground. I believe that education which does not occur through forms of life . . . is always a poor substitute for the genuine reality and tends to cramp and to deaden.
>
> (Dewey, 1897, p. 78)

In the mid-twentieth century, the influential work of Bruner and Bloom placed an emphasis on applying learning across contexts and synthesising (that being, combining and re-applying) knowledge (Bruner, 1962; Bloom, 1956).

This application required the construction of teaching that went beyond ' "telling children and then testing them on what they have been told" to develop motivated learners that actively explore and apply their own knowledge and skills to a variety of contexts' (Bruner, 1962, p. 123).

In most of the qualifications-based curricula – such as GCSEs, Technical Baccalaureate, Extended Diplomas, A-Levels or Foundation Degrees – that students engage with, learning can

Introduction

be explained as multiple focused component parts centred on inquiry, exploring subject matter over time, within a cycle of challenges that are carefully designed and constructed to ensure knowledge and skills that support assessment success.

To meet this outcome, learners' learning should be *applied*; that is, have meaningful real-world contexts and be work-related, where appropriate or possible. This is important (as we shall explore within this book, particularly in Chapter 5) because authentic tasks create a connection for learners with what they know and what they could be, engaging them with their learning to boost their opportunities for successful outcomes.

Professionalism in practice

Consider the subject/s you teach and write a lesson plan that applies the 'medical model' of problem-based learning, focusing on a problem that becomes a case study for your learners to solve through knowledge, finding new resources of credible knowledge and working together. Think of a 'case study', such as:

1 'Why did German society appear to support Hitler's rise to power?' for History or PSHE
2 'What are the main functions of the endocrine system and what happens if these functions fail?' for Biology
3 'Identify and explain the reasons for the most effective sponge recipe' for Hospitality and Catering
4 'What is social enterprise and how can it be successful?' for Business

Consider the following: How would you facilitate the learners in researching the case study? How could you support learners working in groups, to establish a 'solution'? How could you support learners to apply their learning to other subjects or concepts? Could you integrate the use of maths and English?

5

Introduction

Notes on the terms used in this book

In this book, we use the terms:

- *Learner* to describe: any person that might otherwise be referred to as 'pupils' or 'students'. This has been chosen to reflect the wide range of young people that will benefit from applied learning in all educational age ranges.
- *Teacher* to describe: any person that will support the educational and training needs of a learner. This might include teachers, lecturers, trainers, teaching assistants, workplace professionals, or any other professional that is involved in applied learning.
- *Professionalism in practice* to describe opportunities for you to apply the ideas, theories and concepts we have provided to your professional practice.
- *Professional reflection* to describe opportunities for you to reflect on your current practice to develop your teaching, learning and assessment approaches using applied learning.

This positive portrayal of the potential for applied learning in practice should make teachers and lecturers ask why applied learning is not the norm in all classrooms and why so much learning in schools, colleges and universities is not applied to other contexts. We suggest that applied learning involves understanding the purpose, strategies and opportunities; it requires creativity, planning and reflection, which all take time for busy teachers (and is discussed in Chapter 6 and 7). However, we would argue that it is our responsibility to take this time for the benefit of our learners. Our mission statement for this book serves as a reminder of this:

> *We, as teachers, have a responsibility to facilitate learning that not only encourages the traditional application of knowledge and skills, but that also supports learners to develop real-world, future-orientated and independent thought and problem-solving skills.*

Introduction

To support you in developing applied learning in your teaching, we have designed a number of 'Professionalism in practice' sections. 'Professionalism in practice' sections provide opportunities for you to think about what you do in the classroom and how you could start to facilitate a more applied learning approach. There will also be opportunities for you to reflect on your newly applied learning practice, as well as existing practice, through guided 'Professional reflection' sections throughout the book.

References

Bloom, B. (1956). *Taxonomy of Educational Objectives Book 1 Cognitive Domain.* 1979 reprint. London: Longman Group Ltd.

Bruner, J. (1962). *On Knowing: Essays for the Left Hand.* Cambridge, MA: Harvard University Press.

Dewey, J. (1897, January). My pedagogic creed. *School Journal, 54,* 77–80.

Fröbel, F. (1826). *On the Education of Man (Die Menschenerziehung).* Keilhau/Leipzig: Wienbrach.

Stanford University. (n.d.). Problem Based Learning. Retrieved October 2016, from *What is PBL?*: http://ldt.stanford.edu/~jeepark/jeepark+ portfolio/PBL/whatis.html

CHAPTER 1

What is applied learning?

This chapter will:

- explain the concept of applied learning;
- discuss why applied learning is relevant to teaching, learning and assessment today;
- describe how teachers and educators can begin to incorporate some of the underlying concepts of applied learning into their professional practice;
- suggest some prompts for professional reflection.

Applied learning sets learning within practical situations to improve the learner's understanding of how theory works in practice. Ask yourself the following questions and if the answer is 'no' to any of them, then you are already likely to be an advocate for applied learning.

- Would you want to be treated by a doctor who had never practised medicine?
- Would you want a lawyer who had never practised law?

What is applied learning?

- Would you want to be taught by a teacher who had never been on teaching practice?

So why is applied learning important for learners in schools, colleges and universities?

The answer is because applied learning is fast becoming recognised as one of the key approaches needed to meet the needs of the young people today who will live their adult lives in the mid-to-late twenty-first century and into the twenty-second century. While this is a bold claim, it is one that is based on a strong and growing research base, which we will explore in this chapter. However, we must, of course, be cautious about predicting the future needs of young people, and tread carefully when assuming what strategies and approaches will meet those needs.

As Sir Ken Robinson observed in a conference presentation in 2006, "Children starting school this year will be retiring in 2065. Nobody has a clue . . . what the world will look like in five years' time. And yet we're meant to be educating them for it" (Robinson, 2006). However, research into twenty-first century employability and the challenges of teaching and learning for the future are already highlighting applied learning as a secure approach to teaching and learning that is highly relevant to meeting the economic and workforce demands of the future.

For example, the 2016 *CBI/Pearson report* (CBI, 2016) concluded that businesses and employers are looking for two key skillsets in young people: (1) literacy and numeracy, but also, (2) "skills that go beyond academic ability" (CBI, 2016, pp. 31–32). This second category of skills includes communication, problem solving, analysis, resilience and creativity. These are described as "essential skills for the workplace and the rest of life" (CBI, 2016, p. 32). What is most striking is that all of these skills (alongside literacy and numeracy) are effectively and dynamically developed through applied learning.

Similarly, a recent Organisation for Economic Co-operation and Development (OECD) report highlighted the changes and

What is applied learning?

challenges for teaching and learning, with education moving towards teaching for innovation and creativity (OECD, 2012). The report highlighted a framework developed by Charles Fadel, founder of the US-based Center for Curriculum Redesign, as being highly relevant for twenty-first century education. This framework (Fadel, 2015) highlights the importance of:

- *Knowledge – what we know and understand,* where content (curricular) needs to focus more on 'real-life' situations.

- *Skills – how we use what we know,* with teaching of skills integrated into the teaching of knowledge. This is of particular relevance in light of the higher level skills: creativity, critical thinking, communication and collaboration.

- *Character – how we behave and engage in the world,* where development of values is seen as essential for lifelong learning, relationships – within the family and beyond – and participation in the world.

- *Meta-learning (learning how we learn)* – how we reflect and adapt learning.

Each part of this influential framework points towards applied learning as being key and relevant to young people's future work, life, and effective twenty-first century learning experiences.

Defining applied learning

> Applied learning is the development of knowledge, skills and understanding through settings or scenarios that relate to the [employment] sector. It enables learners to develop skills and understanding in a variety of contexts with teachers, other learners and individuals from outside the classroom.
>
> (QCA, 2009, p. 2)

Experiential and active learning are common terms in teaching, and are linked to, and underpin, the ethos and approach of applied learning.

What is applied learning?

Experiential learning

Experiential learning encourages learners to identify the purpose of the task being undertaken, to learn through reflection about how they undertook the task, and then apply (or transfer) this learning to other situations.

Experiential learning is therefore central to successful applied learning. It is an important part of the applied learning cycle. This cycle is a way of ensuring that learning experiences are relevant to learners and contextualised by a journey that takes them from the school/college to a simulated workplace to a real workplace and back to school/college. Figure 1.1 summarises the applied learning cycle.

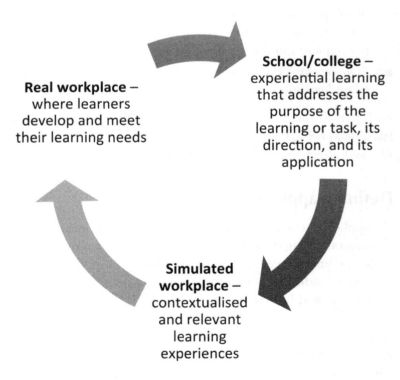

Figure 1.1 The applied learning cycle

What is applied learning?

Active learning

Active learning requires the learner to learn by doing, in order to process skills or information. Active learning can include taking notes, transforming text into a graph, discussing a point with a partner or preparing a presentation. However, all of these activities could be done without thinking about the actual purpose of the learning, or how the learning might be applied to another context.

Active learning can move learners away from being 'passive consumers' of knowledge-based learning towards being 'active explorers' of knowledge, skills and ideas. However, it is important to remember that learners need to be aware of the value of their learning tasks to avoid poor motivation. 'We have constructed ways of being together in formal education that are dull, draining of human creativity, and that fly in the face of intrinsically motivating learning' (Collins, Harkin, & Nind, 2002, p. 167).

Applied learning

Applied learning can simply be defined as: Education put to practical use; learning is *experiential, contextualised* to real situations and *personalised* to the learners' needs.

Effective applied learning brings relevance and meaning to learners through activities that move them from the classroom to the workplace. Activities should centre around real investigation and inquiry, based on contact with working professionals and the roles that they do, wherever possible. Learning should be active, but have a purpose and cross different contexts so that learners can apply knowledge, understanding and skills throughout their lives.

Many learning strategies, such as work-related learning, problem-based learning, creative problem solving and authentic creative challenges can be seen to have elements of, and links to, applied learning. These strategies are often embedded in either experiential or active learning, but the challenge for

What is applied learning?

teachers is to facilitate an appropriate applied learning strategy (or strategies) that has authenticity for the learner and is relevant to the discipline being learned.

Professionalism in practice

Applied learning provides opportunities for learners to take control of their learning. Experiences need to be planned carefully by the teacher, so that learners can make real decisions within parameters of the applied learning activity. Solomon and Rogers, cited in Harkin (2007), conducted a small-scale study of pupil referral units and learner disaffection. They discovered that learners largely felt that learning was something that was done to them and was beyond their control. It is possible to engage learners by giving them more control. Within an applied learning context, this means giving the learner choice and responsibility.

As the teacher you need to manage learners' control and choice. It is worth noting that although it may feel worrying at first to release control to your learners, many teachers report that learners given responsibility in lessons become highly motivated.

Why not give it a go? Identify an element of a lesson you control, such as the plenary, and give your learners the responsibility of designing it from a series of structured options using the principles of applied learning – experiential, contextualised and personalised.

Applied learning and the practice of teachers

In the remainder of this chapter we will look at some of the key aspects of teachers' everyday practice and how this practice can relate to, support or facilitate effective applied learning.

However, it is important to remember that research shows that teachers tend to interpret new learning through previous

What is applied learning?

experience, which is in turn influenced by their personal beliefs and values. The result is that sometimes new ideas that could be beneficial to teaching, learning and assessment may not get the attention deserved and are not implemented as they should be. By making you aware of this possibility, coupled with the fact that you are reading this book, it increases the chance of full engagement with applied learning as an approach for your professional practice.

Applied learning seeks to address the needs of young people in the future, and to establish a more integrated and holistic approach to teaching and learning. This change in approach requires us as teachers and educators to effectively challenge our own assumptions about educational practice. Each of the following sections challenges us to think differently about an area of practice that forms a part of an effective programme of applied learning. A selection of prompts for professional reflection on developing your professional practice can be found at the end of each subsection.

The areas of practice that we will be discussing are drawn from the 2012 OECD report 'Preparing teachers and developing school leaders for the 21st century: lessons from around the world', and are:

- Inquiry-based teaching and learning
- Assessment
- Collaborative learning
- Technology
- Collaboration with colleagues
- Effective school systems.

Inquiry-based teaching and learning

Inquiry-based teaching and learning involves learners applying their knowledge to solve a problem. For teachers, this means enabling and supporting learners to understand the problem,

15

What is applied learning?

consider what they are trying to achieve, establish a way to solve the problem, consider the results (for example, are they what was expected?), evaluate their work and consider any next steps.

For teachers, having a strong knowledge base in the area of learner inquiry is important; providing learners with resources and basic guidance will not be enough. Learners need support on how to use resources, find information, organise and communicate ideas, consider intended goals, assess progress and collaborate with others.

Professional reflection

Key challenges for teachers' practice in inquiry-based teaching and learning include: ensuring that their own knowledge base is up to date and secure; establishing the right balance between support and instruction by scaffolding learner activity; and knowing how and when to 'fade' support and scaffolding to develop independence and autonomy in learners.

How secure do you feel in your subject or topic knowledge? When did you last engage with contemporary research or literature in your specialist subject(s)? Are you relying on vocational experience that is up to date?

What are your assumptions about the concept of inquiry-based teaching and learning? This approach can require a fundamental reworking of the learner–teacher relationship and classroom dynamic. What benefits can you identify? Can you identify any potential negative effects? How might you mitigate these?

What would be the most efficient way to establish the level of support needed by learners as part of your day-to-day practice? Are there any 'non-standard' methods of support that could expand your professional practice? (For example, using online technologies to engage learners outside the traditional classroom or developing peer-mentoring or collaborative working relationships between learners?)

What is applied learning?

Assessment

Learner assessment is a central part of effective teaching and learning. Assessment shows if learning is taking place as intended. When learning is not happening, a teacher can use assessment data (summative assessment) and observations (formative assessment) to make rapid changes to their approach. This is most effective when the teacher knows where the learner is in their learning, where they are going and how best to get there (personalised).

Formative assessment: The goal of formative assessment is to gather feedback that can be used by the teacher and the learner to guide improvements in the ongoing teaching and learning context. Observing learners working during lessons or in placements is a type of formative assessment.

Summative assessment: The goal of summative assessment is to measure the level of success or proficiency that has been obtained at the end of a task, lesson, module, programme or course, and typically includes comparing it against some standardised level or benchmark. An external assessment at the end of a course represents summative assessment, but so too would an in-programme test or problem-based learning (PBL) task. It should be noted that the outcome of summative assessment can be used formatively by teachers and learners to improve on outcomes throughout their programme of study.

Assessment is a cyclical process, which informs long-, medium- and short-term planning. It involves gathering evidence of learners' learning, analysing and evaluating the evidence, and allowing time for teachers (and learners) to reflect on how to develop appropriate and aspirational learning targets. Effective professional practice acknowledges that observing learners first-hand (formative assessment) informs teaching and provides

What is applied learning?

opportunity to develop learning. Developing a framework for common practice across your learners can help to guard against subjectivity in observations; this might take the format of a set of questions, as in the following example:

1   What aspect of learning do I want to assess?
2   What is the best way of collecting this data? (What type of observation?)
3   What outcomes am I looking for?
4   What does the data (my observations) tell me about the learner?
5   What aspects do I need to consider to help this learner develop/progress more independently?
6   How much time do I need to give this learner to develop this skill/progress in this area?

Providing learners with the opportunity to discuss and evaluate (identify the strengths and weaknesses of) their work provides a means of appropriately re-thinking what and how they are learning and is sometimes referred to as assessment for learning. Black and William highlight the benefits for learners, in terms of improved knowledge and understanding, when they have the opportunity to discuss their work with teachers (Black & William, 1998). To be of benefit, assessment needs to be given careful thought that may go beyond common assumptions of the assessment of learner progress. This might include:

- encouraging learners to be involved in their own learning (for example, through inquiry-based learning);
- adjusting teaching practices to take account of the results of assessments;
- recognising the profound influence assessment has on learners' motivation and self-esteem, both of which are crucial influences on learning, and;
- fostering learners' ability to assess their own work and understand how to improve (adapted from OECD, 2012, p. 41).

18

What is applied learning?

> **Professional reflection**
>
> What are your assumptions about the purpose and nature of assessment? Does transferring greater responsibility for learning to the learner (such as in inquiry-based learning) challenge those assumptions?
>
> How do you ensure subjective assessments across your learners? Do you have a standard set of questions? If not, how could you develop these?
>
> How do you ensure that you know where each learner is in terms of their developing learning? How could you better capture this insight to inform support and teaching?

Collaborative learning

Relationships with peers are important motivational and practical factors in learning. In recent years an emphasis on inclusive learning environments has resulted in increasingly mixed ability classrooms and schools. Research indicates that traditional, teacher-directed, whole-class instruction with uniform academic tasks and ways of performing is not always appropriate as it fails to accommodate the differences between learners in terms of their needs and abilities (Ben-Ari & Shafir, 1988).

Vygotsky (1962) emphasised the pivotal contribution of social interaction to cognitive development, and the view that cognitive development is a process of continuous interplay and negotiation between the individual and the environment. It therefore follows that classroom groupings for teaching and peer relationships could have a significant impact on learning. This is particularly relevant to applied learning, where learning experiences may take place in a variety of shifting settings and often in task-orientated groups.

It is important for teachers to recognise and foster the possible mechanisms for improved learning behaviour through

What is applied learning?

collaboration between learners. The lack of appropriate social and inter-personal skills and competencies can result from any background, which makes it necessary to enhance positive learning behaviours in the classroom by encouraging:

1 high feelings of self-worth

2 a robust sense of self

3 self-reliance

4 autonomy

5 a positive view of the world

6 a sense of personal power.

Professional reflection

Do you feel that collaboration between your learners could drive forward learning?

What collaborative approaches do you currently use? How could these be expanded?

How could collaboration between learners improve behaviours for learning? How would you group learners to encourage this?

Technology

Learners in our classrooms today are often the earliest adopters and most fluent users of new technologies. Hand-in-hand with this, technology that would have been the stuff of science fiction 20 years ago is commonplace in our classrooms, for example, the connected classroom that allows us to teach two rooms of learners in different settings miles apart.

However, it is important to bear in mind that access to technology alone is not enough to guarantee high-quality teaching and learning. As long ago as 1990, Terry Mayes (from the Research Centre for Lifelong Learning, Glasgow Caledonian

What is applied learning?

Universities) was placing the role and use of digital technology in education within a wider historical framework (Mayes, 1990). Mayes highlighted the fact that the introduction of most new media (such as radio, film, video, television) was accompanied by a confident prediction that this or that innovation would herald a period of new and more effective educational methods. Mayes argued that these new mediums failed to make the predicted educational impact because their projected use in education was based on a fundamental 'pedagogical heresy', or anti-learning approach. He identified that the possibilities of the new medium was badly presented to teachers, many of whom initially elected not to use these new technologies in their classrooms as they doubted the efficacy.

We argue that the situation today is not dissimilar. The 2012 OECD report cited earlier in this chapter concluded that the use of technology in classrooms across the globe is variable in both application and effectiveness. The OECD highlighted the need for new technologies to be adapted to fit the needs of learners and teachers and not as an end in itself. This is a notable break from historical early thinking on the power of technology. At its most extreme, early thinking on technology in education revolved around two ideas that seem very strange to modern educators.

The first of these ideas was that technology would provide learners with access to bodies of knowledge (in line with the simple view of education as a transmission of knowledge) and, to a greater or lesser degree, overcome the need for teachers. In some ways, this concept continues in a diluted form, with the unimaginable range of teaching materials, lesson plans and resources available 'off the shelf' online being marketed to teachers as time-saving and quality-assured blueprints for successful teaching.

The downside of this type of practice is that teachers and practitioners may not use technology effectively and may lose ownership of both the lesson content and pedagogical design that underpins the classroom activity. The challenge for teachers,

What is applied learning?

particularly when engaged in applied learning, is to ensure that teachers and, crucially, learners develop the skills of informed and critical evaluation of resources and information and apply these appropriately to their own needs.

The second early idea on new technology in schools, colleges and universities was that learners and teachers would have to become 'computer literate'. The writer/actor/comedian Stephen Fry has a parallel career as an informed and deep-thinking historian, advocate and critic of new technologies. In terms of discussing historical predictions for future technologies, he has highlighted many times the widely read *Boy's Wonder Book of Science* from the mid-1930s. This book included an examination of how the latest technology at the time – the brushed DC motor – would revolutionize lives. Fry observed that: 'The piece concluded that, as a result, everyone would be very handy with DC motors – "electric motor literate"', which he equated to the rallying call in the 1990s and early 2000s for 'computer literacy':

> We used to believe that homes would have one great computer controlling music, lights and heating. In fact, we have them in our tumble-driers and thermostats, cars and coffee machines. But we don't have to be computer literate any more than we need to know how a car engine works. All we have to learn is how to negotiate the traffic.
>
> (Fry, 2008)

This is highly relevant to effective teaching, learning and assessment, and particularly applied learning. It can be a conceptual leap for us as teachers to overcome an assumption that so many of us had instilled in us during our own education – that somehow we have to 'learn computers' to effectively use new technology.

In a world where we are surrounded by technology, the need to understand how a digital device works is useful, but subservient to the need to develop the skills and knowledge to effectively and safely deploy those devices. This is as true for the

What is applied learning?

7-year-old learning the fundamentals of coding, as it is for the 16-year-old in a workplace environment learning how 3D printing can support rapid prototyping and product design.

Professional reflection

Early thinking on the use of digital technology in learning, at its most extreme, tended to overlook the role of the teacher. There was talk in the 1990s of connecting all schools via the Internet to a central hub of high-quality resources. It was believed by some that learners would then be able to access these, perhaps with the support of teaching assistants, and thus overcome the need for teachers. Such a view was not new and is based on the assumption that the central purpose of education is the simple transmission of a body of knowledge.

What do you think about this idea? Do you think this idea has relevance today? To what extent does the teacher have a role in supporting learning through technology? Reflect on your use of technology. How could you make better use of technology to improve learner outcomes? Could technology be used to support learners developing independent learning, research, and synthesis skills?

Collaboration with colleagues

Successful provision that ensures that all learners progress and achieve, both in academic and wider outcomes, requires a culture of collaboration with and between staff; with parents or carers; with employers, and often with other agencies. This is clearly part of effective applied learning.

Effective collaboration relies on leaders in and across schools, colleges and universities working together with a sense of collective responsibility for all learners. It also means that leaders are outward facing; looking beyond their own institution, they show an appreciation and understanding that educational

What is applied learning?

organisations may be different, but that strengths and best practice can be shared.

Effective leaders at all levels model shared working practices between institutions and phases of education (NCSL, 2011). This has never been more important, giving the need for the development of skills through education and the merging of the further, higher and compulsory government educational departments in England in the Department for Education (DfE). In addition, effective leaders encourage the development of future leaders.

Professional reflection

How do you, in your day-to-day practice, collaborate with others? This might include how you work with other teachers, parents or carers, employers, or other professionals. Do you take a planned approach to collaboration, or is it more 'as and when'? How could you develop your approach to support the best outcomes for your learners?

How do you develop your leadership skills? Who supports you in this? Where might you be able to get more support, advice and guidance?

Systems for teachers

Teacher effect on learner achievement is well documented in the research literature (Barber & Mourshead, 2007; Chetty, Friedman, & Rockoff, 2011; and Hanushek, 2011). Also, the Sutton Trust report, 'Improving the impact of teachers on pupil achievement in the UK – interim findings' (Sutton Trust, 2011) highlighted the detrimental effect of poor performing teachers on learners' attainment. For those from disadvantaged families, an under-performing teacher can leave the learners as much as 1 year behind in their learning. High-quality teachers are especially

What is applied learning?

important for applied learning, not least because of the transfer to the learner of some responsibilities for their own learning and progress.

Schools and colleges with well-structured systems in place support and enhance teacher development and performance. An example of this is evidenced by the Achievement for All programme implemented in some schools, where systems put in place by leaders, and supported through focused staff professional development, led to improved outcomes for learners (Achievement for All, 2015):

- Teachers being able to take an active role in assessing and monitoring the learners in their class (enhanced through good tracking systems).
- Structured approaches for teachers engaging with parents (enhanced through staff training).
- More personalised approaches to teaching and learning within the classroom (enhanced through peer and senior leader observation of lessons).
- In schools with increased learner attainment and other improved outcomes, teachers being more frequently involved in reviewing individual learner targets (enhanced through regular staff discussion).
- Data-led discussions between the Senior Leadership Team (SLT) and class teachers, providing opportunity to identify learners not making the expected progress and to finding appropriate interventions to help them.
- Teachers planning together for differentiation, allowing for greater focus on individual learners.

Summary

Applied learning is an effective and adaptable approach to learning that research suggests is an effective response to the challenges that today's learners will face in their adult lives.

What is applied learning?

Applied learning requires teachers to challenge their assumptions about their practice, to effectively support and scaffold learning to develop independence in learners, and to work collaboratively across a wide range of partners, including employers, other educators and, most importantly, learners.

In the following chapter we will examine the pedagogy of applied learning, including the concept of a 'teenagogy' and how this can maximise learning opportunities and progress for learners.

References

Achievement for All (2015). Achievement for All impact report 2014–2015. Newbury: Achievement for All.

Barber, M., & Mourshead, M. (2007). *How the World's Best Performing School Systems Come Out on Top*. London: McKinsey.

Ben-Ari, R., & Shafir, D. (1988). *Social Integration in Elementary Schools*. Ramat-Gan, Israel: Institute for the Advancement of Social Integration in Schools, Bar-Ilan University.

Black, P., & William, D. (1998). *Inside the Black Box: Raising Standards through Classroom Assessment*. London: King's College. London: King's College.

CBI. (2016). The right combination – The CBI/Pearson education and skills survey 2016. London: Pearson.

Chetty, R., Friedman, J., & Rockoff, J. (2011). The long-term impacts of teachers: teacher value-added and student outcomes in adulthood. *National Bureau of Economic Research, Working Paper no. 17699*.

Collins, J., Harkin, J., & Nind, M. (2002). *Manifesto for Learning*. London: Continuum.

Fry, S. (2008, September 6). Dork talk. *Guardian*.

Hanushek, E. A. (2011). The economic value of higher teacher quality. *Economics of Education Review, 30, 466–479*.

Harkin, J. (2007). *Excellence in Supporting Applied Learning*. LLUK TDA.

Mayes, T. (1990). *Pedagogy, Lifelong Learning and ICT: A Discussion Paper for IBM Chair Presentation*. Research Centre for Lifelong Learning, Glasgow Caledonian Universities.

NCSL. (2011). *Achievement for All: Leadership Matters*. Nottingham: NCSL.

OECD. (2012). Preparing teachers and developing school leaders for the 21st century: lessons from around the world. Paris: OECD.

QCA. (2009). *Applied Learning Case Studies*. London: Qualifications and Curriculum Authority.

What is applied learning?

Robinson, K. (2006, February). Do schools kill creativity? Retrieved from TED: www.ted.com/talks/ken_robinson_says_schools_kill_creativity?language=en

Sutton Trust. (2011). Improving the impact of teachers on pupil achievement in the UK – interim findings. London.

Vygotsky, L. S. (1962). *Thought and Language* (E. Hanfmann, & G. Vakar, Eds.). Cambridge, MA: MIT Press.

CHAPTER 2

The theory and 'pedagogy' of applied learning

This chapter will:

- explain why applied learning is relevant to teaching and learning today;
- discuss how effective teachers focus on *developing learning* rather than *delivering knowledge*;
- describe how teachers can begin to facilitate high-quality applied learning activities;
- suggest some topics for professional reflection.

As we have discussed in Chapter 1, applied learning is an approach that meets the needs of young learners today as they move into adult life in the twenty-first and, quite possibly, the twenty-second century.

At the heart of applied learning are two key concepts in education: developing teaching strategies that meet the individual needs of young learners (personalised learning); and equipping young people to take an active role in their learning by developing their independent learning skills (metacognition).

The theory and 'pedagogy' of applied learning

Personalised learning

Personalised, or individualised, learning was part of the early twentieth-century move towards the development of education that was 'student or learner-centred' and that sought to support the holistic development of the learner (Dewey, 1897; Piaget, 1951; Vygotsky, 1978; Rogers, 1969). Within a learner-centred framework, a teacher's practice needs to be focused on the needs, progress and development of each independent learner. This practice might include:

- Providing appropriate support that enhances the development of each learner.
- Having, developing and modelling positive attitudes towards diversity and difference.
- Removing barriers to learning, achieving and participating.
- Stretching and challenging all learners.
- Creating and developing partnerships with colleagues, parents and carers, other professionals, schools and other services and provision.
- Enabling learners to develop a love for learning.
- Enabling learners to become lifelong learners.
- Planning for personalised learning, through ongoing and effective assessment.
- Adapting quickly to individual learning needs.
- Promoting the learner's health, safety, emotional and mental health and well-being
- Supporting learners in the development of positive behaviour.
- Managing positive learner behaviour and behaviours for learning.
- Communicating and engaging with learners in an effective manner.

The theory and 'pedagogy' of applied learning

- Sharing information.
- Taking responsibility for continuing professional development.

In applied learning, these practices will provide learners with the context, support and opportunity to confidently 'learn by doing', including the confidence to make mistakes that they will learn from. Crucially, these practices also develop learner security. Learners know that they are supported by teachers and other adults who understand their individual needs and will provide appropriate support and challenge in all of the settings involved in the applied learning cycle (classroom, simulated workplace and real workplace).

Professional reflection

Consider your own teaching practice in relation to the personalised and individual learner needs for development identified above. What could you do better? How could you change your practice?

Independent learning and metacognition

In Chapter 1, we saw how modern employers are increasingly requiring young people who have developed a range of skills in addition to traditional academic capacities. These skills include creativity, problem-solving and what we might call 'self-developmental skills'. Self-developmental skills are those that equip young people to act independently; evaluate their own learning; identify where and what they need to learn to master a task or solve a problem; research knowledge; and develop their own knowledge and skills.

These skills are often described as being part of an individual's 'metacognition'. This describes a learner's understanding of what they have learnt and how to learning. In schools and colleges,

31

The theory and 'pedagogy' of applied learning

learners' metacognition is often developed through a supportive process where the learners are encouraged to find answers for themselves in a safe environment where mistakes are allowed and used to further learning. Often, this approach will include 'fading' support from a teacher to gradually hand responsibility to the learner. This is highly relevant to the applied learning cycle, where the support may fade in a controlled way as the learner moves through the cycle of settings.

Applied learning as a framework that supports the development of independence and metacognition supports the UK government's 2006 vision statement for education by the year 2020 (Gilbert, 2006). This vision included more independent and creative learners who are 'active and curious' and who 'create their own hypotheses, ask their own questions, coach one another, set goals for themselves, monitor their progress and experiment with ideas for taking risks' (Gilbert, 2006, p. 6).

The challenge of applied learning

Developing personalised learning and independent learners through applied learning situations establishes skills for employability and success in the twenty-first century. It is therefore interesting to note that although Stanton (2005; cited in Harkin 2007) suggested that applied learning 'is more complex than academic teaching', it has not received the representation in teacher training or pedagogic research associated with other learning strategies.

This may be because the ideal of applied learning practice falls somewhere between traditional pedagogy (or the 'teacher-centred' model of learning) and a Further Education teacher training model of andragogy focused on the learning of adults (Knowles, 1984).

The developmental maturation of learners preparing for end of key stage 4 and 5 external assessments (14–19-year-olds) crosses the divide between children and adults. On one side of this divide is the idea that children are in more need of direction

32

The theory and 'pedagogy' of applied learning

and control, and on the other side that adults are more self-motivated, can manage their own behaviour and direct their own learning. There is no term to define this transitional phase of learning, but perhaps the teaching of this group could be thought of as 'teenagogy'.

Applied learning provides an opportunity for teachers to facilitate increasing levels of responsibility, choice and autonomy for learners; it provides a potential teaching framework to support a learning journey from child to adult, as outlined in Table 2.1.

Professionalism in practice

Use Table 2.1 to consider your own experiences of teaching learners between the ages of 14 and 19 years of age. Evaluate the accuracy of the 'teenagogy' column in relation to your own experiences. Write down what you feel is appropriate to add or take away from the common features of the teenage learning experience. Discuss this with your colleagues, other professionals and your teenage learners.

Why are teenagogy and applied learning so important?

In their research of the learning experiences of 14–19-year-old learners, Lumby and Foskett (2005) concluded that these learners were regarded and taught as school children. It appeared that teachers found it easier and safer to control a class engaged on the same activity, seated in the classroom, than a class all engaged on different projects working at the pace relevant to individual progress. The risk of traditionally 'pedagogic' approaches to learning is that they can restrict independence and lead to greater learner disaffection.

Table 2.1 Pedagogy, andragogy and teenagogy

	Pedagogy	Andragogy	Teenagogy
The learner	The learner is dependent upon the teacher for all learning. The teacher assumes full responsibility for what is taught and how it is learned. The teacher evaluates learning.	The learner is self-directed. The learner is responsible for his/her own learning. The learner is required to reflect and self-evaluate.	The learner is facilitated in learning by the teacher. The learner has some control over what and how they learn. The learner learns how to reflect and how to self- and peer-evaluate.
Role of the learner's experience	The learner comes to the lesson with little experience that could be utilised as a resource for learning. The experience of the teacher is most important.	The learner brings experience to the lesson. The learners are a rich and diverse resource for one another.	The learner's prior knowledge, understanding and skills are articulated. The learners are a resource for one another.
Readiness to learn	Learners are told what they have to learn by the teacher in order to advance to the next level.	Learners are ready to learn. Learners have a real-life reason to learn. Learners can identify what they need to do to be successful in learning.	Learners are ready to learn when shown the purpose, direction and relevance of learning. Learners can identify what they need to do to be successful in learning.
Orientation to learning	Learners are taught prescribed learning materials on the subject. Learning materials are structured for the learner in the perceived to be appropriate order.	Learners want to perform a task and solve a problem. Learning must have relevance to real-life tasks. Learning is organised around life/work situations.	Learners are supported by teachers. Learners want to perform a task and solve a problem. Learning must have relevance to real-life tasks.
Motivation for learning	Learners are primarily motivated by external pressures (extrinsic motivation), competition for grades, and the consequences of failure.	Learners have internal motivation (intrinsic motivation) related to self-esteem, recognition, better quality of life, self-confidence, self-actualisation.	Learners have both intrinsic and extrinsic motivation.

The theory and 'pedagogy' of applied learning

It is also notable that, despite nearly a century of research, theory and practice, which has consistently highlighted the value of learner-centred approaches to teaching (such as social constructivism and humanism), pedagogical and behaviourist views of teaching continue to be regarded by many sections of the educational establishment as being the 'common sense' default teaching approach (see 'Concepts and theories explained', below).

Secondary education in England is constantly under scrutiny from educators, media, government and employers. In 2006, the Leitch Report considered the education and skills shortage (Leitch, 2006). Only 83 per cent of 17-year-olds in the UK, compared with 90 per cent in the best-performing countries, were engaged in education and one in six learners left school with inadequate literacy and numeracy skills. Many of these learners are capable of succeeding in education, but are not motivated to do so. The report concluded that reform in the education system was required to increase retention and to equip learners for a rapidly changing world.

Whatever new qualifications and curricula are devised by successive governments, applied learning as a teaching strategy addresses these issues, whether formally laid out in qualifications labelled 'applied' or not. The current government control of educational qualifications with the move to a knowledge-based curriculum, externally assessed and synoptically devised (Department for Education, 2016) suggests a more traditional, didactic approach to teaching and learning would provide greater learner success. However, we would argue that there is even greater reason to engage learners with applied learning, as this is the only means to develop transferable skills; skills essential in a twenty-first century global economy.

It is important for teachers to remember that if their learners understand what they are learning, why they are learning it, how to develop their learning, the relevance of this learning to the real world and how to apply it across contexts, then their learners will be motivated to learn.

The theory and 'pedagogy' of applied learning

Concepts and theory explained

Pedagogy derives from the Greek 'paidagogia' – 'paid' meaning child and 'agogos' meaning leader. Thus, pedagogy originally meant education, attendance on children. The teacher-centred model has been central to the pedagogical model. The teacher, according to this model has full responsibility for making decisions about what will be learned, how it will be learned, when it will be learned, and determining if the material has been learned. Pedagogy, therefore, places the learner in a submissive role.

Andragogy is a term created from the Greek word 'andros' meaning man and 'agogos' meaning leader, but is used to refer to the teaching of adults. The term 'andragogy' was originally formulated by a German teacher, Alexander Kapp, in 1833. However, Malcolm Knowles introduced the term (then spelled 'androgogy') in 1968 and developed a theory of adult learning education in 1970.

Behaviourism focuses on teacher and learner behaviour, with learning occurring as a result of transmission of knowledge by the teacher to the learners (Skinner, 1972; Bandura, 1986). The goal is to achieve exemplary outcomes for learners through expert teacher knowledge and clear 'rewards' (good and bad) for learners as a system of control. For 14–19-year-olds, learning would be through more didactic strategies, which ensure that the expert teacher is in control of the learning experience.

Social constructivism is a psychological school of thought that describes how learning happens through the process of thought. The theory of constructivism suggests that learners construct knowledge out of their experiences and it is often associated with pedagogic approaches that promote active learning or learning by doing. Piaget (1951) and Vygotsky (1931) offered theories that identified stages at which the maturation of the learning would enable more complex types of learning. For the 14–19 age range, learning would be at a 'formal operational level' (Piaget, 1951) of logical hypothesising and learners in the Zone of Proximal Development (ZPD) where maturation of ability to learn independently is well developed (Vygotsky, 1978).

The theory and 'pedagogy' of applied learning

Teachers are facilitators and learners participate actively in in constructing meaning about what they are learning.

Humanism values the emotional and developmental needs of the learner above all other things (Rogers, 1969; Maslow, 1943). Learning will occur in an environment of trust, where the teacher acts as facilitator for the learner's own learning needs and ambitions. Students aged 14 to 19 years old are considered eager to learn and should be given responsibility for directing their own learning, with teachers facilitating this process by listening to their learners' feelings and encouraging them to self-evaluate. An interesting example of a humanist approach in compulsory schooling is Summerhill School, an independent British boarding school that was founded in 1921, which holds the belief that the school should be made to fit the child, rather than the other way around.

Professionalism in practice

Does your classroom offer learner choice and responsibility?

The best Design Technology classes are a good example of where applied learning allows for independence of thought and movement.

A group of learners may all be working on different projects, supported by the teacher who responds to the needs of individuals as they arise. They may have already had specific skills lessons on the key aspects of the project, but learners understand the health and safety aspects and use the resources and prior learning to apply skills and knowledge to their own design.

Practical subjects provide clear examples of applied learning because the outcomes are more clearly visible and observable. Transferring the application of algebra or poetry analysis into a meaningful context will take more consideration, but will be worth the effort to support learner engagement and the development of transferable skills.

The theory and 'pedagogy' of applied learning

Using applied learning approaches to meet the challenges of teenagogy

In this section, we will examine how applied learning can be used to develop an effective teenagogy that addresses some common issues encountered by teenage learners.

Removing barriers to participation, learning and achievement

Enabling learners to take ownership of their learning is key to their participation, progress and achievement.

Teachers need to promote positive attitudes to learning, which will help learners to develop the confidence and belief in their competencies needed to actively participate in their learning. The development of positive attitudes in young people is predominantly dependent on teachers creating a learning context and environment that supports and promotes 'independence'.

Enabling young people to progress and recognise their progress means paying close attention to the holistic development of the learner. The pedagogical model of didactic teaching can tend to consider this form of development as being less important than the development of bodies of knowledge. However, applied learning, with its focus on 'learning by doing' and a different learner–teacher dynamic, can play a key role in developing the whole learner.

Some examples of how applied learning can increase participation are included below, informed by some key aspects of the personalised learning framework developed by Cheminais (2006):

- Enable the learner to know that you have high expectations because you know he/she can achieve. For example, by ensuring that the learner is fully aware that any workplace learning experiences have been designed to challenge but also to support the learner to achieve.

The theory and 'pedagogy' of applied learning

- Start from the learner – build on his/her *knowledge, interests and aptitudes*. For example, by offering individualised applied learning experiences that build on and stretch the learner.

- Plan for learning – develop a repertoire of strategies, pacing the learning experience to make it *challenging and enjoyable* for each learner. For example, by ensuring that workplace learning experiences are as carefully planned and paced as any classroom-based or simulated workplace-based experiences.

- Involve learners in their own learning – share *objectives and feedback*. For example, by ensuring that the learner is: involved in setting their objectives for workplace-based learning; aware of the criteria for assessing their progress, achievement and areas for development; and provided with high-quality formative feedback that provides them with both independent and teacher-supported next steps in learning.

- *Inspire learners* – enable them to see/experience your passion for learning. Modelling a passion for learning is a basic skill of every effective teacher, but in applied learning situations, teachers can also ensure that any other professionals in classroom or workplace contexts are aware of how inspirational seeing passion for learning can be.

- Enable learners to become *confident, co-operative learners*. For example, by providing opportunities for learners to work collaboratively together in problem-solving activities or peer-support roles, and by providing learning contexts where mistakes and set-backs are valued as learning opportunities.

- Consider progression – enable learners to *develop the skills* they will need beyond school and college. For example, by working closely with any workplace settings to ensure that the learning that takes place is relevant, rigorous and grounded in real life (adapted from Cheminais, 2006, p. 42).

39

The theory and 'pedagogy' of applied learning

Stretching and challenging learners

Various learning and teaching strategies have long been associated with challenging and stretching young people; including effective questioning and the development of thinking skills through purposeful reflection.

In practice, and particularly in terms of applied learning, this means having a structured, well-thought-out approach to each learner's learning needs. As we discussed earlier, personalised learning is essential for effective applied learning.

The word 'challenge' is too often used in educational circles, with little attempt to explain what it means in practice. The online Oxford Dictionary defines it as: "A task or situation that tests someone's abilities. . . . Invite (someone) to do or say something that one thinks will be difficult or impossible. . . . Make demands on; prove testing to" (see: www.oxforddictionaries. com). Although these definitions provide some insight into the 'practice' of 'challenge', they still leave much open to interpretation and the initiative of the teacher.

In practice, stretching and challenging learners in applied learning situations is dependent on both the learners' individual capabilities and informed and realistic teacher judgements of those capabilities. Challenge requires careful thought both in planning for learning and on a moment-by-moment basis when supporting learners in their learning experiences. This is especially important in workplace learning situations where the teacher may not be immediately available to rework their planning for learning, or to make on-the-ground instant changes.

In practice, teachers using applied learning strategies will need to strike a balance between:

- Helping learners to engage fully with an activity and develop the skills and confidence to think through problems and find possible solutions;

- Knowing when and how to personally intervene with appropriate support;

40

The theory and 'pedagogy' of applied learning

- Spending time and energy in ensuring that other professionals engaging with the learner (for example, in a workplace setting) are able to offer consistent and professional support to the learner.

Meeting learners' individual needs

Individual learning can place the teacher at the centre not of a single model, but of 20 to 30 models of learning, depending on the number of learners the teacher is engaging with at any given time. To design a curriculum that responds to individual learning needs requires detailed knowledge of the learner, the subject matter and a clear understanding of the teaching input and support that is required.

This is especially important in applied learning situations where it may take imagination and effort to ensure that familiar and effective structures of teaching and learning are maintained in any non-classroom context(s).

To provide broad and varied learning experiences, teachers will also consider the wider academic, social, developmental and emotional needs of individuals. To put it simply, teachers must ensure that learners have every opportunity to achieve. The wider 'teenagogical' aspects of applied learning can be a real benefit to teachers in this respect; being naturally more aligned to 'real-life' situations and experiences.

Teaching in applied learning contexts should recognise and strive to maintain the social elements of traditional educational settings that prepare learners for life in adult society. Applied learning approaches should provide opportunities for learners to frequently interact with both adults and their peer group.

Irrespective of teaching and learning content or style of delivery, there is an ethical, values-led purpose to education. What happens in an applied learning situation should enhance the capacity of young people to learn, their learning behaviours, and their motivation to learn. If this happens, learners succeed and are initiated into lifelong independent learning for their own development and self-efficacy.

The theory and 'pedagogy' of applied learning

In essence, the characteristics of effective applied learning that meets individual needs are:

- Equipping learners to question and challenge (for example, to ask why something happens/to think of alternative solutions to problems/to question why something worked/did not work).

- Supporting learners to make connections and see relationships, both in terms of concepts or ideas, and with other learners and professionals.

- Giving learners the opportunity to envisage what might be (for example, by helping learners to be creative, not only in 'creative endeavours' such as art or music, but in their problem-solving and day-to-day lives).

- Learners, teachers and other professionals exploring ideas, and reflecting on ideas, actions and outcomes.

An effective teacher is a skilled leader of environments for learning. This is as true for a teacher working in applied learning contexts as it is for a teacher in a 'traditional' classroom. For this reason, it is fundamental that teachers should have the ability to plan, select and arrange activities.

Planning appropriate learning experiences is the central skill of teaching, and of managing applied learning. When considering the appropriateness of the applied learning activities offered, it is important for the teacher to be able to predict learner responses, reactions and pace of work and progress.

Teachers and other professionals working in applied learning contexts need to be consistent. In particular, this means having specific, shared and expressed expectations of the learners. Within the applied learning offer, teachers and other professionals must be constantly alert to the learning content and the wider opportunities for learners, and be able to identify and select concepts and tasks that can be used to stretch or challenge learners when necessary.

The theory and 'pedagogy' of applied learning

Creating independent learners

To achieve their full potential, learners need to be appropriately supported in environments that nurture talent. Applied learning is ideally placed to provide these environments. However, while it is widely acknowledged to be self-evident that supporting learners will promote and enhance their development, there is no general consensus as to how or when teachers and other professionals should intervene. This is as true for applied learning as it is for 'traditional' learning contexts.

Independence in learning does not mean leaving learners to manage their own learning; rather it means knowing when to initiate or direct learning, when to prompt or intervene and when to remain on the 'outside'. In applied learning contexts, this also includes, crucially, sharing and developing these subtle but profound teaching skills with the other professionals and adults that support and engage with the learner.

Professionalism in practice

Bloom (1956) developed an idea about learning, commonly referred to as 'Bloom's taxonomy', which divided learning into three separate sets of skills or domains – cognitive (thinking), affective (social, emotional) and psycho-motor (physical). The taxonomy has generally been regarded as a hierarchy, taking learning from basic to high level skills.

However, in terms of supporting learning in applied learning contexts, it may be more useful to think of learners taking a journey through a range of skills that become progressively more complex.

For example, if we consider Bloom's taxonomy within applied learning for teenagers, we could start by assessing our learners' prior knowledge, skills, learning skills, motivation and relationships with peers, teachers and others, and personalise their experiential learning accordingly to ensure that their 'journey' is appropriate.

43

The theory and 'pedagogy' of applied learning

> **Professional reflection**
>
> In this chapter, we have examined some of the research and theory which suggests that traditional approaches to pedagogy may not meet the learning needs of young people who will live their adult lives in the twenty-first century.
>
> We have suggested that there is a gap in practice between pedagogy and andragogy and proposed the need for a concept of 'teenagogy'. We have argued that teenagogy can be actualised through applied learning. We have briefly looked at how applied learning can address some of the common issues associated with ensuring effective learning, particularly in the 14–19 age range.
>
> It would be disingenuous of us to suggest that some of the ideas we have presented do not challenge 'traditional' teaching practice and learning management. In particular, this includes advocating a transfer of increasing amounts of responsibility to the teenage learner to manage their own learning experiences, independence and metacognition.
>
> Reflecting on these ideas, what is your view on the need for a 'teenagogy'? How relevant do you feel this concept is to your teenage learners? How do you think you could develop your applied learning practice to meet the needs of learners in the 14–19 age range?

Summary

Applied learning can be a powerful tool to develop independent learners, who are equipped to understand their own knowledge and to be active partners in the development of their ongoing learning. Applied learning achieves this by establishing the learner's individual needs and putting in place learning opportunities to meet these needs.

We have also argued that applied learning can act as tool to 'bridge the gap' between 'child-relevant' pedagogy and 'adult-relevant' andragogy, acting as a key component of the concept

The theory and 'pedagogy' of applied learning

of a 'teenagogy' that meets the specific needs of 14–19-year-old learners preparing for external assessments.

In the following chapter, we will examine the key aspects of applied learning in teaching practice.

References

Bandura, A. (1986). *Social Foundation of Thought and Action: A Social Cognitive Theory*. Englewood Cliffs, NJ: Prentice Hall.

Bloom, B. (1956). *Taxonomy of Educational Objectives Book 1 Cognitive Domain*. 1979 reprint. London: Longman Group Ltd.

Cheminais, R. (2006). *Every Child Matters: A Practical Guide for Teachers*. London: David Fulton.

Department for Education. (2016). *Educational Excellence Everywhere*. London: DfE.

Dewey, J. (1897, January). My pedagogic creed. *School Journal, 54*, 77–80.

Gilbert, C. (2006). *2020 Vision: Report of the Teaching Learning in 2020 Review Group*. Review Group. Nottingham: DfES.

Harkin, J. (2007). *Excellence in Supporting Applied Learning*. LLUK TDA.

Knowles, M. (1984). *Andragogy in Action*. San Francisco: Jossey-Bass.

Leitch, S. (2006). *Review of Skills Prosperity for all in the Global Economy – World Class Skills*. Final Report. London: The Stationery Office HMSO.

Lumby, J., & Foskett, N. (2005). *14–19 Education Policy, Leadership and Learning*. London: Sage.

Maslow, A. H. (1943). A theory of human motivation. *Psychological Review, 50*(4), 370–396.

Piaget, J. (1951). *The Psychology of Intelligence*. London: Routledge and Kegan Paul.

Rogers, Carl (1969). *Freedom to Learn*. Columbus, OH: Charles E. Merrill.

Skinner, B. (1972). Utopia through the control of human behavior. In John Martin Rich, ed., *Readings in the Philosophy of Education*. Belmont, CA: Wadsworth.

Vygotsky, L. S. (1931). *The Collected Works of L. S. Vygotsky: Vol. 4. The History of the Development of Higher Mental Functions* (M. Hall, Trans.; R. W. Rieber, Ed.). New York: Plenum Press.

Vygotsky, L. S. (1978). *Mind in Society: The Development of Higher Mental Process*. Cambridge, MA: Harvard University Press.

CHAPTER 3

Applied learning in teaching

This chapter will:

- explain some of the key aspects of teaching in applied learning contexts;
- discuss what applied learning looks like in practice;
- describe how good practice in applied learning requires good practice in teaching;
- suggest some prompts for professional reflection.

In the previous two chapters we have examined how applied learning can inform high-quality and relevant teaching practice that enables teachers and other professionals to improve the achievement and progress of learners.

We have discussed how the concept of applied learning is based on providing all learners with rigorously relevant contexts and authentic learning experiences that are informed by an understanding of: the personalised needs of learners; the contexts that these learners will experience in their future adult lives; and evidence-based, high-quality educational practice.

Applied learning in teaching

This chapter will turn to exploring what applied learning looks like in terms of day-to-day practice for teachers.

What applied learning means in practice

For teachers, effective applied learning practice requires best practice in teaching and will crucially include:

- Knowing learners and how they learn as individuals.
- Having high aspirations for the progress of learners.
- Providing learners with ownership of their learning.
- Taking a personalised approach to the starting points, learning journeys and target-setting of learners.
- Carrying out relevant and regular assessments of learners, and keeping good records of these to inform learner support and development.

These practices are actualised by schools, colleges and universities that:

- have clear and appropriate assessment systems in place that are learner focused;
- have known and agreed policies for marking and feedback;
- have open and structured monitoring and evaluation approaches for all processes and practices.

For learners, effective applied learning practice enables access to:

- the curriculum, the programme of study, and the subject in its widest sense;
- support from teachers and other professionals who will establish confidence, aspirations and opportunities to learn;
- enhanced outcomes through the increased independence of a personalised, experiential and authentic learning experience;
- learning opportunities that develop high self-esteem and self-mastery skills.

48

Applied learning in teaching

The implementation and development of applied learning through high-quality teaching is centred on a set of key effective practices:

- Engagement of learners (which is enhanced by the engagement of their parents or carers, if appropriate, and linked to learning that is 'real' and relevant to the learner).
- Effective assessment (measurement of progress through data tracking, target setting and development of learning opportunities).
- Appropriate teaching strategies (approaches that support authentic learning relevant to the topic, which encourage a personalised approach and support independence in learning.
- High aspirations for learners (which are consistent across their learning experience in the institution).

When there is a rigorous and institution-wide approach to these key practices, the progress of young people is significantly improved. It is, however, important to remember that putting in place these practices requires full institutional involvement (Coe, Aloisi, Higgins, & Major, 2014). For the teacher, it has been argued that their practice should focus on six common areas for achieving effective teaching:

- Subject knowledge;
- Quality of teaching;
- Classroom/setting climate;
- Classroom/setting management;
- Teacher beliefs; and
- Professional behaviour (adapted from Coe et al., 2014, pp. 3–4).

In practice, these areas will be encountered differently in the classroom, workplace settings, and across the school, college and university. However, to support an applied learning approach a teacher should provide opportunities for learners that are REAL

Applied learning in teaching

– Relevant, Engaging, Active Learning – and grounded in solid subject knowledge to facilitate growing independent learning in a safe and constructive environment, which is inclusive and builds confidence to achieve.

Quality teaching can help learners surmount intergenerational barriers to learning, but the particular approaches and strategies for each episode of applied learning need to be embedded into the regular practice and culture of the institution. When considering the six areas of quality teaching outlined by Coe et al. (2014), the synergy between the elements is a key consideration. All of the areas are interlinked. For example, teacher beliefs will underpin effective professional behaviour; effective professional behaviour will increase learners' aspirations and develop positive learning environments; good subject knowledge will increase the quality of teaching; improved quality of teaching will increase learner outcomes and experiences.

To make any change to practice requires the teacher, and other professionals, to 'take ownership' for change. Teachers' sense or 'feeling' of responsibility for the learning and achievement of learners in their class can be the axis on which the quality of teaching turns. Research evidence (such as Humphrey & Squires, 2011) suggests that when teachers are given responsibility for their learners and learning in their classroom by senior leaders, and provided with focused training, learner academic and wider outcomes are significantly improved.

A case study example in practice: Film School

Film School is a project run each year by the Cornwall College Camborne Media Department to create a realistic practical working environment for media and music technology students. Film School involves students generating original ideas for a film script, devising all aspects of pre-production, shooting, editing and creating sound effects and music for a finished short film. Learners then produce a marketing package and pitch the whole project to industry experts for feedback – all within a

Applied learning in teaching

2-week period. The finished film is then premiered at the internationally recognised Cornwall Film Festival.

The intense nature of the project creates a frenetic environment that generates innovative ideas and drives motivation. The normal timetable for these learners is suspended and they focus solely on this activity with the support of industry experts and their tutors for a concentrated period. Film School takes place in a dedicated production office that recreates a realistic working environment and takes learners away from the comfort zone of the classroom. The imposition of short deadlines reinforces this setting.

Extended Diploma vocational students flourish when given access to genuine work experience opportunities that enable them to see what their chosen industry is really like. Media production in Cornwall is often carried out by relatively small independent producers, which means industrial work experience opportunities tend to be scarce. In response to this, the teachers at Cornwall College Camborne decided to establish an alternative work experience provision and Film School was born.

Rory Mason, the teacher responsible for implementing the 'exploded curriculum' that is Film School, states:

> The Film School Project creates a learning environment and work ethos that would be impossible to create in the classroom setting. Working with industry professionals to extremely tight deadlines outside of the usual teaching space generates a unique experience that enables students to gain a valuable insight into the actual workings of the different production roles required to complete a short film.
>
> The Film School Project over the last 2 years has dramatically increased the learners' involved motivation and dedication. Retention and achievement are excellent and the students now have a real ambition to successfully complete the course and go onto Higher Education and then the industry.

For further information see: https://www.cornwall.ac.uk/news/students-get-film-studio

Applied learning in teaching

We have argued in this book that applied learning must support a growing independence in learning for the learner, as independent learning demonstrates an intrinsic motivation to self-develop. Educational institutions can do the same for teachers, with leaders giving more responsibility and autonomy to teachers to decide how their learners learn most effectively. This can be a challenging proposition in systems that are judged by external performance measures, but small steps towards enabling teachers to take professional control over their practice can be made as follows:

- Teachers take an active role in designing internal assessment for learners (which might include enabling learners to co-construct their own assessment) and monitoring their progress.

- Teachers become central in reviewing individual learner targets (which supports an understanding of the learner for a more personalised approach).

- Teachers engage in data-led discussions with the Senior Leadership Team (SLT) (which provides opportunity to identify learners not making the expected progress and finding appropriate, maybe REAL, interventions to help them).

- Teachers plan with other teachers, and other professionals such as Teaching Assistants, for differentiation and applied learning (which supports a greater focus on individual learner needs and sharing of best practice through collaboration).

- Teachers undertake subject and pedagogic continual professional development (CPD) (which increases teacher knowledge and skills, resulting in more effective teaching and learning within the classroom) (adapted from Humphrey & Squires, 2011).

Professional behaviours linked to professional development are most effective when they include not only the development

52

Applied learning in teaching

Professionalism in practice

It is useful when planning an activity or task to map Functional Skills (FS) against all that the learners do (see Chapter 5 for more information on Functional Skills and the role they continue to play in supporting applied learning and the wider programme of study in Further Education). Whilst Personal Learning and Thinking Skills (PLTS) no longer play a role in the National Curriculum, they can still be a useful map for considering the nature of episodes of applied learning. You can use the following key to identify PLTS and FS for strategies 3–10 in Table 3.1:

Personal Learning Thinking Skills (PLTS):

✓ Independent Learners (IL)
✓ Creative Thinkers (CT)
✓ Team Workers (TW)
✓ Effective Participators (EP)
✓ Reflective Learners (RL)
✓ Self-Managers (SM).

Functional Skills (FS):

✓ English (E)
✓ Mathematics (M)
✓ Information Communication Technology (ICT).

of teacher skills, but those of parents and carers for learners up to 19 years of age. Parents are enabled to become 'real' partners in their son's or daughter's education, contributing to accelerated progress. This is more challenging depending on the parent's or carer's own educational experiences and the expectations they have of education for transforming their child's opportunities. Intergenerational unemployment or low employment can impact on parental/carer belief in education to provide future employment and this can lead to disengagement with the child's learning experience (Ovenden-Hope & Passy, 2015).

Applied learning in teaching

High standards of behaviour are achieved across classrooms when learners feel valued and want to be part of their institution (Passy & Ovenden-Hope, 2016). The quality of interaction between teachers and learners as well as teacher expectation is enhanced by addressing effective communication and interaction skills across the curriculum. In helping young people to develop as independent and confident learners, teachers and other professionals need to give particular attention to the creation of a positive environment. A stimulating learning environment, including workplace settings and simulated workplace settings, will produce high-quality results.

Coe et al. (2014) were critical of praising learners as a means of encouraging learning and progress. They suggested that it may inhibit further development by inadvertently giving out the message 'this is the best you can ever be'. However, appropriate feedback and praise for those vulnerable to underachievement is vital; teachers and other professionals need to avoid putting them into a situation where they become the 'forever failures'. This is particularly important in a context where families do not have belief in education to change personal and social circumstances. It also demonstrates why it is so important for the teacher to know their learners as individuals. Only by understanding who the learner is – their background, their aspirations – can the teacher hope to find an effective teaching approach to engage them in learning.

For those who have a history of low attainment, learning can be supported by breaking it down into small sections with appropriate feedback provided at regular intervals; learners need to develop confidence in themselves and in their abilities to learn. This involves 'enabling' an internal change in the learner, supporting and encouraging them to develop a positive disposition to learning and achievement. Applied learning is particularly effective in supporting previously low attaining learners, when teachers:

54

Applied learning in teaching

- make learning REAL (Relevant, Engaging, Active Learning) through real-world tasks and problems, which helps learners to fully understand the purpose of their learning;

- refine their teaching strategies to engage every learner in the class or workplace setting (focusing on what, how, when and why can support this refinement);

- ensure that tasks, projects and content curriculum are interesting, and challenge learners to both achieve and accept mistakes as an opportunity to learn through doing again.

This last point is important for developing autonomous learning in all learners. If teachers are to support learners in developing independence, metacognitive and transferable skills, these learners must be aware of their own gaps in understanding, knowledge and skills and their ability to fill these gaps themselves (with support from the teacher as necessary).

Applied learning is ideally suited to meeting the needs of all learners, not only those who may have had previous low attainment or those aiming for vocational qualifications or apprenticeships. Applied learning provides REAL opportunities for learners from which they can build their knowledge and understanding of the world in which they live, and develop the essential skills to be successful in it.

The next sections of this chapter will explore some strategies that can be used by teachers and other professionals to engage applied learning in teaching.

Applied learning and teaching strategies

You will apply different teaching strategies throughout a lesson, workshop or programme. It is possible to use lectures, demonstrations, active and kinaesthetic learning, and collaborative learning (strategies 1–4 described in Table 3.1) without the learners applying their learning or moving beyond 'knowing'

Applied learning in teaching

or 'understanding'. It is possible, however, that by adding higher order thinking to active learning and collaborative learning, the activities could utilise applied learning.

Table 3.1 provides two simple 'subject' examples (one practical/vocational and one theoretical/academic) to explore different teaching and learning strategies from both the teacher's and learner's perspective:

- Learning how to make the beverage, tea; and
- Learning about the trade union movement.

Applying learning in academic subjects, where the majority of knowledge comes from reading about concepts and hearing them explained, can be achieved by contextualising beyond theory into creative problem solving, requiring learners to explain and evaluate beyond original knowledge.

On a psychology course, for example, a teacher may ask the learners to use their knowledge of different theorists' perspectives on psychology and adapt this for a work-related area that is relevant to them, such as public services, thereby making the theory relevant to their interests. This would require the learner to understand the knowledge, analyse it, synthesise it and evaluate the outcome.

Professional reflection

We have explored a number of strategies where applied learning can meet the needs of learners.

How do you feel about these approaches? Do they challenge your assumptions?

What could you do to develop your practice? What support might you need to engage with these approaches?

56

Table 3.1 Applied learning strategies

Teaching and learning strategy	Example teacher activity		Example learner activity
1. Lecture	a)	Teacher talks about how to make tea, may use visuals and sound stimuli, for example, PowerPoint.	Learners listen (maybe taking notes).
	b)	Lecture on the history of trade unions and industrial action.	
2. Demonstration	a)	Teacher talks about how to make tea and demonstrates tea-making process.	Learners look and listen (maybe taking notes).
	b)	Teacher talks about the history of trade unions and industrial action by showing historical media footage.	
3. Active and kinaesthetic learning (only applied if part of strategy 5–10)	a)	Teacher talks about how to make tea and demonstrates sets tasks on tea-making to engage learners.	a) Learners look, listen, draw flow charts and write instructions.
	b)	Teacher gives learners historical resources on trade unions and industrial action with a series of comprehension questions to answer and report back.	b) Learners make notes and share findings.
4. Collaborative learning (only applied if combined with 5–10)	a)	Teacher sets task on how to make tea.	Learners undertake tasks in groups and present findings to class.
	b)	Teacher gives each group a different historical topic on trade unions to research and present findings.	
5. Applied learning	a)	Teacher organises a tea-tasting party with local food expert on the theme of teas from around the world. Provides resources and references to research the teas.	a) Learners use instructions to make and serve each other tea and research information on the different teas for a display, which illustrates the geography and the time periods involved.
	b)	Teacher sets the task of planning the setting up and running of a trade union challenging an employer on equal pay for women.	b) Learners study early trade unions and role they play in negotiations with an employer.

6. Work-related learning	a) Teacher sets a task to plan training for staff in a tea shop that sells and serves tea to make the most efficient use of time and space and serve hot tea.	a) Learners consider all factors, experiment with ideas and produce a plan that is simulated in the classroom.
	b) Teacher invites a union representative to plan an equal pay case relating to a real union with the learners.	b) Learners present their case to the teacher in role as the employer.
7. Authentic learning	a) Teacher organises a day in an old people's home, or in the staff room, for the learners to prepare tea for residents/staff.	a) Learners make and serve tea to clients in the real setting.
	b) Teacher helps learners consider a real-life current issue that relates to trade unions and industrial action that will have an impact on them, which they research and report on.	b) Learners research the current situation and debate the likely outcome based on historical precedent.
8. Problem-based learning	a) Teacher sets a tea-related problem that draws out the learning in the learner, e.g. which material used for tea bags makes the best tasting tea? Which lasts longest in the cupboard? How long does it take to biodegrade?	a) Learners work with a set of provided materials to conduct their own investigations and find their own solutions/outcomes.
	b) Teacher identifies problem resulting in industrial action, such as an airline crew strike as a result of changes in pay and conditions, which the learners must resolve with minimum impact to service.	b) Learners must resolve the problem, and negotiate from the employer's perspective, losing the minimum amount of money (short and long term) without disrupting services.
9. Creative problem solving	a) and b) Teacher negotiates a problem with the learners, with multiple potential outcomes, in an aspect of the topic that interests them.	a) and b) Learners plan and develop their own projects on the topic.
10. Authentic creative challenge	a) and b) Learners identify with the teacher a real-world opportunity to solve a problem or achieve a challenge that addresses the demands of the topic, e.g. to promote green tea to young people as a source of antioxidants; or how to ensure low paid workers join a union for job protection.	a) and b) Learners plan and execute the project to a challenge with a real-world context and with an audience beyond the classroom or workshop.

Summary

Applied learning in practice is directed and enabled by a number of factors that include: curriculum content; teaching approach and strategy; the involvement of a number of professionals and institutions; professional behaviour; assessment practice; and the knowledge, approach and values of teachers and educators.

Effective practitioners of applied learning regard challenges to their assumptions and approaches to be positive and regular events.

In the following chapter, we will examine the requirements and form of applied learning in practice.

References

Coe, R., Aloisi, C., Higgins, S., & Major, E. (2014). *What Makes Great Teaching? Review of the Underpinning Research.* London: Sutton Trust.

Humphrey, N., & Squires, G. (2011). *Achievement for All National Evaluation Interim Report 2 (RR123).* Nottingham: DFE Publications.

Ovenden-Hope, T., & Passy, R. (2015). Changing cultures in coastal academies. Cornwall: Plymouth University and The Cornwall College Group. Retrieved 1 April 2015, from https://www.cornwall.ac.uk/sites/default/files/documents/Coastal%20Academies%20Report_2015_final_2%20Tanya%20Ovenden-Hope%20and%20Rowena%20Passy.pdf

Passy, R., & Ovenden-Hope, T. (2016). Changing student behaviour in schools located in areas of socioeconomic deprivation: Findings from the 'coastal academies' project. *Education Today, 66*(3).

CHAPTER 4

Applied learning, employment and employers

This chapter will:

- explain why applied learning is relevant to work-related and vocational learning, and how employment-based settings and partners can contribute to this;
- discuss how effective teachers develop *effective applied learning*;
- describe how teachers and other professionals can construct high-quality applied learning activities;
- suggest some topics for professional reflection.

Applied learning and skills for employment

This chapter will examine two key approaches in teaching practice for employer engagement in applied learning:

1 Mentoring; and
2 Team-working/team-building.

It will also discuss three areas for developing learners' skills for employment:

Applied learning, employment and employers

1 Work-related learning on non-vocational/academic courses;
2 Work-related learning on vocational courses; and
3 The role of employer engagement.

Applied learning: Aspects of teaching practice for employer engagement

A landmark report from the Higher Education Academy (Kettle, 2013, p. 4) defined employer engagement in the context of work-based learning as:

> a range of activities, initiatives and approaches which are best conceptualised as a continuum. It includes responsive teaching and learning developments for upskilling and developing people already in work as well as fostering capability and attributes to enhance the employability of students in higher education.

This report highlighted the complexity of employer engagement with education and proposed a number of flexible teaching strategies in the delivery of learning.

When teachers are deciding on the most effective learning strategies to use for work-based learning, the Kettle report suggests the following questions as a useful framework for decision making (Kettle, 2013, p. 42):

- Who will deliver the learning and how will they be supported?
- What kinds of learning approaches and tools will you use and why?
- How important is flexibility for learners?
- How important is flexibility for employers?
- What evidence are you drawing on to know what employers and learners want in terms of flexibility?
- What are the restraints on your approach?

Applied learning, employment and employers

- How influential is the pace and the place on the methods chosen?

- What makes it a flexible approach?

Teachers should give time and consideration when planning employment-based learning opportunities, as these can provide REAL opportunities for learners that will contextualise any classroom learning previously experienced.

This section will now consider two teaching approaches – mentoring and team-work/team-building – in terms of how these can help to improve employability of the learner and/or develop their professional and/or academic knowledge.

Mentoring

Mentoring essentially means positive and ongoing support offered by one experienced person to another less experienced person. In terms of professionals engaged in delivering applied learning, this will usually be in the form of one teaching professional with solid experience supporting another professional involved in teaching who has less experience of the area being developed. The experience of the first teacher can extend over a wide range of activities, or be specific to one activity.

Mentoring approaches will differ according to need, but will normally include:

- Developing the mentee's (i.e. the person being mentored) skills and professional development;

- Helping to develop the mentee's set of educational values;

- Consulting with the mentee to help them to clarify goals and ways of implementing them;

- Helping to establish a set of personal and professional standards and expectation; and

- Establishing and nurturing networking for the mentee, by providing opportunities for the mentee to meet, and learn from, other professionals.

Applied learning, employment and employers

Although effective mentoring is time consuming, it provides a highly effective approach to professional development as teachers have REAL opportunities to progress in their practice. It is for these reasons that mentoring works well for learners in supporting applied learning work-related experiences. Mentoring should be a continuous activity that becomes part of day-to-day thinking for development. Therefore the mentor and mentee partnership, whether this is teacher to teacher development or learner to employer support in the workplace, has to be the right fit. Any element of judgement in mentoring should be avoided, as the relationship will only flourish to develop learning if built on trust and respect.

Mentors need to know, understand and practise essential elements of a mentoring relationship, which include:

- A recognised procedure for engagement and contact, whether formal or informal.
- A clear understanding of the procedure and the roles of mentor and mentee.
- Trust and a rapport between both parties.
- The credibility and genuineness of the mentor as perceived by the mentee.
- Confidentiality and discretion.
- A relationship based on the mentee's perception of his/her own needs.
- A suitable range of skills used by the mentor: counselling, listening, sensitive questioning, analysis and handing back responsibilities.
- An appropriate attitude by both parties, for example, the ability of the mentor to challenge the mentee, and the self-motivation of the mentee to take action when necessary.
- In addition, teachers should be aware of equality issues that need to be addressed in the selection and training of mentors, to avoid unconscious bias and promote diversity.

Applied learning, employment and employers

Developing strong mentors from employment to support learners in developing employability skills and specific workplace knowledge can be challenging. The essential elements for successful mentoring identified above demonstrate that planning mentoring into a programme is crucial, as the recruiting, training and monitoring of the mentors will be time consuming. However, as with praxis-based learning discussed in the Introduction, mentoring is also part of the training of most 'hands-on' professions, such as medicine, construction or teaching. Learning with an expert in a real-life setting builds knowledge, understanding and skills; as well as confidence to do the job right.

Professional reflection

How might you establish and sustain an effective mentoring system for learners engaging in the workplace?

You may wish to consider the particular opportunities and challenges of a workplace setting in terms of how, when, where and how often mentors and mentees will meet and interact.

Similarly, you may find it useful to reflect on which aspects of professional practice could be focused upon to best meet the mentee's professional learning needs, and the wider needs of the learners.

Team-working and team-building

In developing effective teams of teachers and other professionals working for applied learning, careful consideration needs to be given to the fact that teams do not act as teams simply because they are described as such. Everard, Morris, and Wilson (2004) defined a team as:

> A group of people with common objectives that can effectively tackle any task which it has been set to do. The

Applied learning, employment and employers

contribution drawn from each member is of the highest possible quality, and is one which could not have been called into play other than in the context of a supportive team.

(Everard et al., 2004, p. 163)

Team leadership has attracted many commentators and academics. Northouse, an author in the field of leadership relating theory to practice, emphasised the need for team leaders to focus on 'what makes teams effective or what constitutes team excellence' (Northouse, 2004, p. 210). He suggested that leaders cannot improve groups without a clear focus on team goals or outcomes and proposed the following considerations for developing an effective team:

- *Clear elevating goals* – the team should be kept focused on goals that are increasingly challenging and outcomes should be evaluated against these.

- *Results-driven structure* – teams should establish the best structure to realise their goals.

- *Competent team members* – team members need to be provided with the appropriate information and training to carry out their role effectively and to enable them to work collaboratively within the team.

- *Unified commitment* – involving team members in the various processes of 'business' can enhance the sense of unity and therefore success.

- *Collaborative climate* – teams should be founded on trust to develop honesty, openness, consistency and respect, enabling individuals to share ideas and work together for the common goals.

- *Standards of excellence* – expectations of team members need to be clearly articulated and reviewed, with clear feedback on progress and outcomes and the acknowledgement of superior performance.

Applied learning, employment and employers

- *External support and recognition* – teams must be provided with the necessary resources to carry out the required tasks and rewards related to team performance, not individual performance.

- *Leadership of effective teams* – leaders influence teams through four processes: cognitive – help the team to understand the problems faced; motivational – unites the team to achieve the required standards; affective – supports the team in coping with difficult situations by providing clear goals, assignments and strategies; and co-ordination – matches individual skills to appropriate roles, provides clear objectives, monitors feedback and adapts to changes (adapted from Northouse, 2004, pp. 211–215).

Building the team

Developing team skills will involve a balance between concern for the team, concern for the task and developing the individual. Few leaders are able to achieve this effective balance. Everard et al. (2004, p. 163) highlighted the 'ineffective way tasks are handled' when teams do not 'gel' and, referring to educational settings, they further suggested that: 'when ... groups ... fail to work at peak efficiency the effectiveness of the whole organisation suffers'.

A leader may find identifying the characteristics of his/her team to be a difficult task. The nature of the task and the ethos of the setting will influence the working habits of team members. Equally, pressure from external agencies will affect the quality of the team. Family commitments, hobbies and political initiatives are areas of influence on leaders' lives; these, in turn, will influence the individual's commitment to the team. In essence, the quality of the relationships within the team will determine the quality of the task.

Those who participate in effective teams should agree on aims, share skills, realise potential and reduce stress and anxiety.

Applied learning, employment and employers

A leader should avoid the pitfalls of weak management, which include:

1 over-emphasis on people;

2 over-emphasis on task;

3 over-emphasis on agendas, not processes;

4 reacting to events, not anticipating them; and

5 failure to celebrate success, the individual and the team.

Essentially, successful team-work depends on a clearly defined set of aims and objectives, the personalities of team members and the team leader. Team-work is, as with all aspects of effective leadership, time-consuming. Now consider the teachers' expectations of the learner to work in teams, to lead teams and generally engage in team-work. Having discussed the challenges for effective team-working and team-building, the success for young people as part of a team can be supported by the teacher through careful planning of the learning process.

The teacher, in establishing clear aims, objectives, roles and ways of working, must also *build* that team. Figure 4.1 sets out the progressive stages of team-building identified by one of the leading figures in the science and art of building teams, Bruce Tuckman (1965).

The complexity of the team leader's role is further illustrated by West-Burnham's nine components of team effectiveness (in Coleman & Bush, 1994), which are explained as:

1 *Explicit and shared values* – No team can operate effectively unless it is working in a context where the values are clear and agreed, and translated into a mission.

2 *Situational leadership* – The team is sufficiently mature to base leadership on function and needs rather than power and status. Skills are more important than hierarchical factors. This requires a willingness by the designated leader to stand back and allow other team members to assume control according to the needs of the situation.

Applied learning, employment and employers

FORMING

The team is not a team, but a set of individuals.
The focus is on the team purposes, composition, leadership and life-span.
Individuals are concerned to establish their personal identities in the team
and make some individual impression.

STORMING

Having reached a consensus on the team's purpose, conflict arises as assumptions
are challenged. Personal agendas are revealed and some inter-personal
hostility may be generated. Successful handling enables the team
to reach fresh agreement on purpose, procedures and norms.

NORMING

The team seeks to establish its norms and practices: when and how it should work.
As working procedures are established there will be a communication of feelings,
mutual support and sense of team identity.

PERFORMING

Solutions to problems emerge, the team is mature and productive.
Individuals and team are relaxed and confident.

Figure 4.1 Tuckman's (1965) stages of team-building

3 *Pride in the team* – This implies commitment and involvement and is manifested in high morale and loyalty. Team members have self-belief, and confidence in others and the team as a whole.

4 *Clear task* – The outcome that the team is created to achieve is clear, realistic and understood. Teams are motivated by tangible goals, clear outcomes and a firm time-scale.

5 *Review* – Effective teams learn and develop by a process of continuous feedback and review. Team review is a

Applied learning, employment and employers

permanent feature of every activity and leads to more effective working.

6 *Openness* – Teams achieve a high level of candour in review and exchange. There are no 'hidden agendas' and there is praise and criticism. The latter is frank and direct, but constructive rather than negative.

7 *Lateral communication* – Team members are able to communicate with each other without reference to the team leader. Networks are formed and nourished by the team.

8 *Collaboration* – Decisions are shared and have full commitment. Quality decisions emerge from the full utilisation of the knowledge and skills of team members.

9 *Action* – Team decisions are expressed in terms of action. Each team member knows what has to be done, by whom and when. Effective teams issue agreed actions after their meetings (adapted from Coleman & Bush, 1994, pp. 279–280).

Motivating teams

Perhaps the most important element of team leadership is the ability to motivate others. Team members who are motivated and committed create an environment that motivates and inspires learners. Leaders who know and understand how to motivate teams will enable colleagues to develop professionally; teachers who know how to do this will inspire their learners in achieving success.

Team leaders should create conditions that focus on opportunities to achieve high standards and meet all goals. A leader should encourage participation and facilitate team-work. A team leader will serve as a role model to his/her team members. Stoll, Fink, and Early (2003) suggest that 'one of the most powerful ways leaders can lead others' learning is through modelling' (Stoll et al., 2003, p. 122). In practice this will require leaders of teams in applied learning situations to:

Applied learning, employment and employers

- provide participants with challenges and intellectual stimulation;
- celebrate the positive impact teachers are having on learners;
- practise participatory decision-making or co-construction of learning;
- encourage collegiality and collaboration;
- develop positive appraisal or reporting systems;
- enhance individuals' self-esteem;
- articulate performance expectations; and
- be aware of and use the rewards that staff members value.

Clearly motivation is more than satisfaction; it also requires knowledge and understanding of what is expected, and sharing a common goal that is highly valued by the team.

Applied learning: Areas for developing learners' skills for employment

Work-related learning on non-vocational courses

Work-related learning implies a direct relationship with the world of work and links with employers, professional bodies and business practices. You can read about the workings of an engine, or watch a demonstration of the workings of an engine, but it is only when you work on an engine that you start to see whether the knowledge you have developed has been understood and has a practical application in a real-life situation.

Applied learning requires some independence on the part of the learner and the development of creative, reflective and team working skills. Applied learning expects the teacher to teach, facilitate, mentor and use skilful formative and summative assessment strategies to support individual development in both generic and subject-specific skills.

Applied learning, employment and employers

If we take the example of a Geography A-level task, learners may be asked in an applied learning strategy to review the local area in relation to designating land for building additional housing, which is a genuine local issue being addressed by the council. Learners are presented with the issues by a planning officer and they develop questionnaires, run a survey and present findings to the council. This kind of learning highlights the need for skills such as networking with professionals, communication and liaison with employers and working effectively as part of a group.

This one example shows that a teacher will be required to establish a bank of professional contacts to support applied learning in their subject area. It can be a challenge; it is a reason why a teacher may choose more traditional learning approaches, however institutions may already have established employer links. The Local Enterprise Partnership (LEP), Chamber of Commerce or school/college/university department that supports employer liaison may all have access to already established educational employer engagement.

Making learning work related will not only highlight learners' transferable skills, but will ensure learners are more employable. Employability skills, whether taught as a separate course or embedded in our repertoire of teaching skills, are important to 14–19-year-old learners.

A case study example of practice: Deloitte employability skills

The Deloitte Employability Initiative is deliberately designed to sit alongside students' vocational courses, and participants on the employability course range from bricklayers, hairdressers, chefs to business students (for further information see http://qualifications.pearson.com/en/qualifications/btec-workskills/the-deloitte-employability-initiative-in-partnership-with-pearson/about.html).

Applied learning, employment and employers

The Deloitte course is designed to promote job readiness, teaching learners vital employability skills, helping them learn and demonstrate the capabilities and attitudes that will support them in succeeding in employment, while making an immediate contribution to their employers. The course enables students to develop a range of skills including CV writing, team-building, leadership and running events within their local community, mock interviews, networking, and analysis, problem-solving and improving first impressions. Essential to the course is self-assessment, ensuring students are able to identify their strengths and weaknesses so that they can mature and improve their abilities.

Learners are also able to gain their 'Young Leaders in Service' Gold Award through the Deloitte programme, which is recognised internationally and is an added bonus to include on their CVs (as well as assisting with UCAS applications).

The Deloitte programme works well in both Further Education and school settings. Learners in school enjoy the various work-related activities and events that they get involved in and help to organise, which develops their confidence exponentially. A really good example can be seen with the Macmillan Coffee Morning (a charity money raising event) with the added twist of a careers fair. The learners are tasked with organising the coffee morning event within a framework of requirements that includes raising money for charity and inviting local and national employers to come into their school for the morning to provide a careers fair for the year 11s to 13s. This works well because the learners are in control (independent and responsible), they feel more relaxed about speaking to employers because the conversation is focused on the event, they develop self-esteem through the acceptances of employers to participate and through the other learners' engagement, and their teachers and employers feedback about their performance.

During the course of the Deloitte programme, the learners evaluate their performance, identifying: various skills they have developed; what they have achieved as an

Applied learning, employment and employers

individual and within a team; what they consider can be improved on; and realistic targets, which they set themselves. Teachers have reported that as the learner's confidence grows, so does their positive mind-set and aspirations for the future.

Alice undertook the Deloitte programme and below shares part of her application for Deloitte Student of the Year, which she won based on her growth as a learner and potential for successful employment:

My name is Alice and this is my journey . . . I'm 19 years old and currently living in Cornwall while I'm studying at Cornwall College, doing both an Extended Business Diploma and Level 2 and 3 of Deloitte Employability. I started Cornwall College in 2013 and, since then, I have dramatically grown as a person and developed an extensive range of work and life skills. I am an extremely passionate and motivated individual and continuously want to push myself towards greater opportunities. I believe that you have to work hard for success; it doesn't happen on its own.

At the beginning I wasn't the strongest member of our course, but the desire to be successful was always on my mind. Throughout the 2-year period and with the help and support of Employability Level 2 and 3, I have come to realise my full potential and ability. By end of my course in 2015, I have grown into a mature young adult and my self-confidence has rocketed.

My future aspirations
In the coming years, I want to further develop my skills and education at University by studying Accounting and Finance at UWE Bristol, as this is a great passion of mine. Following this, I hope to participate within the Deloitte Graduate Scheme after I have completed my degree.

Alice's teachers agree with her self-evaluation. Sandie Johns, Lead for Deloitte in Cornwall College, demonstrates the value of applied learning in the way that Alice has developed as a learner:

Applied learning, employment and employers

> Alice has developed a good work ethic, problem-solving skills and quality of focus with regards to her work. Alice is resilient, adaptable and has a good professional mind-set. Alice is able to plan and prioritise her work, has a good financial acumen understanding and is able to manage working in unfamiliar environments. She is innovative, has a good career direction ambition (Deloitte Graduate Programme), and is able to reflect and review on her own performance along with her team's performance and Alice does this by using a critical analysis approach.

Work-related learning on vocational courses

Vocational courses lend themselves more easily than academic courses to work-related learning as the sector skill focus is already at the centre of the programme. Learners apply the skills they have learned on the course to a real-life, work-related situation. The learners apply their knowledge exactly as they would in a paid work situation under the supervision of the teacher.

A useful example of work-related learning can be seen in an FE College that runs a small restaurant, staffed by learners, and which is open to the public. Using skills that learners have developed on a catering course, they plan and deliver a three course meal with silver service to paying customers.

Preparing the learners for this experience might involve role play to establish appropriate customer relations when dealing with enquiries and complaints, and planning and executing a menu to a time schedule. Learners may also be given specific dietary needs of customers as a problem-solving activity, adapting recipes and menus.

Applied learning, employment and employers

Professionalism in practice

Are you up to date with the range of employment in your sector and the qualifications, skills and experience your learners will need to successful enter their chosen employment?

Are you aware of Apprenticeships and their role in post-16 training and skills? Could you support a learner looking to move to an apprenticeship? Could you identify trailblazers for your subject area?

Do you know the relevant sector skills council? Can you access their website for current information to support learners looking for employment in that area?

Does your college/school/university have existing industry/employer/business contact/s with whom you can work? Who are they and what are their contact details?

Employer engagement

Many employers will be happy to work with you and your learners providing they can see a benefit to their company. You might have experienced this from the employer's side in a previous career and will know how important it is to establish good relations. Ideally you will want to work with an employer more than once and there will be protocols in your institution that will help this, such as only one person contact an employer from the institution to avoid oversaturation of request.

The most important thing to instil in the learners is that employers are usually doing the school, college or university a favour and that they should be polite, attentive, interested and friendly. They might even make a contact and get a job out of a work experience or work-related opportunity.

Applied learning, employment and employers

> **A case study example for practice**
>
> A 14-year-old learner made links with the Royal Shakespeare Company (RSC) on Tour as part of school work experience.
>
> The work experience contact was sustained over the years when the learner later trained as a stage manager with the RSC and was employed directly by them 8 years later.
>
> The school that the learner attended has tracked the progression of the learner and realises the very strong link they now have with the RSC for future employer engagement. This demonstrates an effective employer engagement model and highlights the importance of tracking learner progression into employment.

There are many ways you can work with employers to enhance applied learning, such as:

- Inviting professionals into your institution (or even better, let the learners invite them in) to give presentations about their role, company etc.

- Asking businesses to host visits for learners.

- Inviting employers to contribute to the design of modules, or topics within them (something that was established explicitly with Foundation Degrees, to ensure that degree level learning was relevant to employment on graduation).

- Requesting examples of working practice, such as 'agile' working in the digital technologies industry, that can be shared practically with learners.

- Establishing regular employers' participation in learner assessment, for example, watching presentations and providing feedback from an industry perspective.

Applied learning, employment and employers

There will be school, college or university protocols on employer engagement that you must adhere to, paying particular attention to safeguarding children and vulnerable young adults.

While good employer engagement can be time-consuming, developing good relations with business and industry should be seen as a long-term investment that will improve outcomes and opportunities for learners.

A case study example of practice

The 'Sharing Practice' area of the Education Scotland 'Partnership for Learnings' website (Education Scotland) includes a description of a focused and imaginative applied learning project undertaken by learners at the Sir E Scott primary and secondary school, which serves the whole of the Isle of Harris and Scalpay. At this school there are approximately 50 primary and 112 secondary pupils.

Full details, including video clips and transcripts, can be found at the Education Scotland website: www.educationscotland.gov.uk/resources/practice/e/sirescot tschool/introduction.asp?strReferringChannel=learningandte aching&strReferringPageID=tcm:4-616171-64

Harris Tweed Hebrides is the major employer in the local area. The school partners with Harris Tweed Hebrides provide learners with opportunities to work with the business to develop an understanding of the multiplicity of skills required for self-employment.

This is contextually important as the modern weaving industry is driven by self-employed workers. Learners work with Harris Tweed to develop their own designs, focusing on skills in design, mathematics and ICT, and to understand the opportunities and challenges of self-employment.

The partnership has led to the development of a recognised qualification (a National Progression Award in Harris Tweed). Education Scotland concludes that:

> The award also involves effective partnership working. Young people work closely with local weavers in a work-related setting and within the classroom. They

Applied learning, employment and employers

have been involved in the whole process of weaving from gathering the wool and delivering it to mills, to involvement with weaving workshops, to the sale and export of the finished product.

This has given the young people a valuable and informative insight into how a business operates both at local and global level (including the pros and cons of self-employment) from product design to finished article, and has enabled the young people to have a 'hands on' experience with real-life employers. It has also raised awareness of a cultural heritage that spans hundreds of years, and of an industry that was the livelihood of many of the young people's forefathers.

Professionalism in practice

A teacher of a Creative and Media Diploma course utilised a local and a popular environmental educational tourist destination to develop an applied learning assignment.

The learners visited the tourist attraction and were given a tour of the gift shop by the company. The learners were then briefed by the tourist destination staff on their challenge, which was to develop ideas for sustainable products to sell in their shop, which they would be expected to pitch to the 'client' in 10 weeks.

The learners worked in groups (supported by their teacher) in planning and designing their ideas and then producing prototypes. The learners returned to the tourist destination with their product ideas ready to pitch to members of the company's staff.

The learners were given full feedback from the tourist destination, which they used to evaluate their own performance and outcomes. One product idea was good enough to be developed by the company and is now on sale at the gift shop.

- Plan an activity that engages a local employer and uses the principles of applied learning for your subject area. Remember to keep it REAL – Relevant, Engaging, Active Learning.

Applied learning, employment and employers

> **Professional reflection**
>
> Consider the relationships you currently have with your team(s), colleagues and external organisations (such as employers). Are you making the fullest possible use of these relationships to develop opportunities for learning? What elements of these relationships could you use to support applied learning?

Summary

Effective applied learning requires clear and consistent approaches to developing relationships (with employers, and other educators), and high-quality teaching practice and employer engagement for developing employability skills in learners.

Professional relationships in business are built of effective team-work and building teams is complex and time consuming. Learners are expected to work in teams and strategies for engaging and motivating them in preparation for work are discussed.

Learners' skills for employment require teachers and their team(s) and other related professionals to think widely and imaginatively about the engagement with employment and how to support the progress and success of learners. Establishing high-quality engagement from employers is essential in applied learning.

In the following chapter, we will examine how teachers facilitate applied learning through specific examples.

References

Coleman, M., & Bush, T. (1994). Managing with teams. In T. Bush, & J. West-Burnham, *The Principles of Educational Management*. Harlow: Longman.

Applied learning, employment and employers

Education Scotland. (n.d.). Entrepreneurial skills – Sir E Scott School. Retrieved from Education Scotland: www.educationscotland.gov.uk/resources/practice/e/sirescottschool/qualifications.asp?strReferringChannel=learningandteaching&strReferringPageID=tcm:4-616171-64

Everard, K. B., Morris, G., & Wilson, I. (2004). *Effective School Management* (4th ed.). London: Paul Chapman Publishing.

Kettle, J. (2013). *Flexible Pedagogies: Employer Engagement and Work Based Learning*. York: The Higher Education Academy.

Northouse, P. (2004). *Leadership: Theory and Practice*. Thousand Oaks, CA: Sage.

Stoll, L., Fink, D., & Earl, L. (2003). *It's About Learning (and it's About Time): What's in it for Schools?* London: Routledge Falmer.

Tuckman, B. W. (1965). Development sequence in small groups. *Psychological Bulletin, 63*(6), 384–399.

CHAPTER 5

Facilitating applied learning

This chapter will:

- explain how effective practitioners facilitate applied learning;
- discuss nine key factors that underpin good facilitation of applied learning;
- describe what teachers do in practice to realise the greatest possible impact of applied learning;
- suggest some topics for professional reflection.

There are many factors that influence and impact on the ability of teachers and other professionals to facilitate applied learning, however, we consider the following nine factors key in supporting teachers facilitating applied learning opportunities:

1. The role of the teacher
2. Inclusive practice
3. The teacher–learner relationship
4. Increasing aspiration and access

Facilitating applied learning

5   The learners' mindset

6   Collaborative learning

7   Problem-based learning

8   Functional skills

9   Health and safety.

The role of the teacher: What does a teacher *do* to facilitate applied learning?

In the previous chapters, we have considered key elements that contribute towards and principles that guide an applied learning experience. Now we need to explore what the teacher actually has to do in the classroom, or work setting, to facilitate applied learning.

The start of the learning journey has to be with the learner and the teacher will first need to take into account and *use prior learning*. The teacher will need to find out what the individuals in the group know, what they can do (skills) and the standard or level at which they are working. Prior learning can be assessed in a variety of ways, for example, by using recorded data on achievement; or the learner can be asked as an individual or as part of a group. Understanding learners' prior learning means that the teacher can plan for personalised stretch and challenge, while supporting areas for development in relevant, engaging and active ways.

Engaging learners is very important and can make the difference in them becoming lifelong learners or not. To fully engage a learner in the learning experience the teacher will need to *share learning outcomes* for the programme, course or module at the beginning of the learning experience. Learners will also want to know how these outcomes will be assessed and expectations for deadlines in achieving them. When considering how to facilitate this in an applied learning approach, think of how to support learner independence by providing flexibility

84

Facilitating applied learning

of opportunity through learner choice in what and how learners are assessed.

Constructing a scheme of work and/or lesson plan *with* your learners can be a valuable step in facilitating applied learning, as it brings the learner fully into their own learning experience. You are building their investment into the course by enabling learners to feel that their opinions and choices matter. Below is a checklist that may prove useful when planning a lesson or module that uses applied learning.

Checklist for applied learning lesson

- What skills and knowledge relating to the curriculum do I want the learners to apply?
- What skills and knowledge do the learners feel they want to develop?
- Are these existing or new knowledge and skills? If existing, can they be consolidated through building on prior learning?
- How will I ensure that learners have learned the basics of the necessary skills and knowledge?
- What task/s will facilitate the application of skills?
- Will there be an element of learning the skills within a wider challenge?
- Will I need to run some skills lessons to include use of equipment and resources?
- Do learners have any preferred learning styles? As individuals? As a group?
- Are there any health and safety implications?
- Can I involve employers or other members of the community to enhance the lesson?
- Can I include an element of co-construction and invite learners to plan the lesson with me?
- Are the learning outcomes, assessment criteria and any deadlines clear to the learners?
- Is the lesson inclusive, relevant, engaging and active in the learning taking place (REAL)?

Facilitating applied learning

> **Professional reflection**
>
> Considering the checklist above, how much of your current practice takes these issues into account? How could you work (ideally with other professionals) to develop your practice to take into account an applied learning approach to lesson planning?

Inclusive practice

Teachers are responsible for facilitating the development of knowledge, skills and values for learners; values that include notions of inclusion and lifelong learning modelled and embedded throughout the learning process.

Stainback, Stainback, Esat, and Sapon-Shevin (1994) suggest that 'the goal of inclusion is not to erase differences but to enable all students to belong within an educational community that validates and values their individuality' (p. 489).

Teachers and other professionals typically work together as a team and when facilitating applied learning it is vital that the team agrees on and implements positive conditions for learning and development for all learners (as discussed in Chapter 4). These positive conditions also need teachers to consider learners as a whole in relation to the curriculum (both formal and informal) and their other learning experiences. To sustain the highest standards in practice, inclusion is best understood in terms of what it means and what it aims to do within the context of practice.

In 2015 the Centre for Studies on Inclusive Education (drawing on the work of Booth & Ainscow, 2011) explained what inclusion in education means:

- Putting inclusive values into action.
- Viewing every life and every death as of equal worth.

Facilitating applied learning

- Supporting everyone to feel that they belong.
- Increasing participation for children and adults in learning and teaching activities, relationships and communities of local schools.
- Reducing exclusion, discrimination and barriers to learning and participation.
- Restructuring cultures, policies and practices to respond to diversity in ways that value everyone equally.
- Linking education to local and global realities.
- Learning from the reduction of barriers for some children to benefit children more widely.
- Viewing differences between children and between adults as resources for learning.
- Acknowledging the right of children to an education of high quality in their locality.
- Improving schools for staff and parents/carers as well as children.
- Emphasising the development of school communities and values, as well as achievements.
- Fostering mutually sustaining relationships between schools and surrounding communities.
- Recognising that inclusion in education is one aspect of inclusion in society.

(Centre for Studies on Inclusive Education, 2015)

The role of the teacher or any other education professional is fundamental to fostering understanding of inclusive thinking and practice within the team(s) they operate in, and in the wider educational community. In doing so, it is necessary that teachers have an understanding of the opinions, attitudes and experiences of colleagues, learners and parents/carers. Julie Allan, currently professor of Equity and Inclusion at the University of Birmingham, argued in 2003 that: 'Becoming inclusive . . . means

87

Facilitating applied learning

> **Professional reflection**
>
> Consider the above list of what inclusion in education means (CSIE, 2015). Do you think it would be possible to create an inclusive learning community in your educational setting if all teachers and other professionals did not share these values or principles? Why or why not? What challenges may be posed if values and principles are not shared?

becoming political; listening to what children and their parents say about what inclusion means to them; and recognising the way in which we ourselves are implicated in practices that exclude' (Allan, 2003, p. 178).

Since the 1960s, classroom practice has been influenced by the child-centred theories of thinkers such as Piaget (1951), Montessori (1966) and Fröbel (1826). These theories have emphasised a focus for teachers to reflect on the needs of the learner in approaches to learning and teaching. The initial challenge of this focus is how to make education more responsive to the individual and how to deliver personalised learning. As we have explored previously, this is also the key challenge of effective applied learning.

A comparative review of innovation in learning environments across OECD countries and economies (OECD, 2005) highlighted the importance of putting learning at the centre of learners' own development. Learning was recognised as social and collaborative and effective when learners were engaged and able to understand their own learner needs. In this environment teachers are required to be:

- highly attuned to learners' motivations and the importance of emotions;
- acutely sensitive to individual differences, including in prior learning;

88

Facilitating applied learning

- demanding of every learner, without overloading learners;
- applying assessments that emphasise formative feedback; and
- promoting connections across activities and subjects, both in and out of the school, college or university.

Developing good learning relationships is fundamental to effective teaching. However, it is vital to remember that these relationships are factors within a 'classroom' or other learning environment rather than being sets of attributes of a learner (Cornwall & Tod, 1998). Essentially, the social context and dynamics of the classroom (and the importance of wider social influences on learners' behaviour) should not be ignored.

Case study research suggests that the quality of the relationship between teacher and learner is very significant (Cline, 1992). Stoll, Fink, and Earl (2003) advocate *'positive relationships* as a *secure basis for learning'*. Earlier research (Serrow & Salomon, 1979; Prawat & Nickerson, 1985) suggests that young people and learners are more likely to develop positive attitudes and behaviours when they experience positive relationships with their teachers.

The self-perception of a teacher about their knowledge and skills establishes their confidence as a practitioner and is an important consideration for the management of relationships in the classroom. If a teacher lacks confidence in their ability to teach effectively, it has the potential to impact not only on learning outcomes, but on behaviour and engagement of learners.

Active learning of the kind that we see in applied learning is to be encouraged. However, if learners are to be motivated and take responsibility for their own achievements, they will have to be self-motivated and collaborate with others to construct their knowledge. Moll and Whitmore (1998) describe the teacher's roles (which are highly relevant to applied learning) as 'guide and supporter, active participant in learning, evaluator and facilitator'.

89

Facilitating applied learning

All of these roles are part of the relationship between teacher and learner, but there are many less definable or measurable facets to the relationship that are equally important in facilitating applied learning, such as the ability to encourage and motivate the learner. Castelikns (1996) uses the term 'responsive instruction' for teacher behaviour typified by availability and willingness to:

- support and instruct;
- take the learner's perspective on work problems;
- support the learner's competencies;
- challenge the learner to be active and responsible in choosing, planning, executing and evaluating the activity and its outcomes.

Involving learners in the planning of their learning objectives or goals has benefits to learners that range from ownership of targets to more accurate judgements or assessment of their own performance (Munby, 1994). To achieve this kind of learner involvement there must be an encouraging and trusting relationship between teacher and learner.

Relationships with peers are also important for effective learning. In recent years an emphasis on inclusive environments has resulted in increased mixed ability classes. As we have discussed earlier, research indicates that traditional whole class, teacher-led instruction with uniform academic tasks is inappropriate, as it fails to cope with the differences between learners in terms of needs and abilities (Ben-Ari & Shafir, 1988).

Vygotsky (1962) emphasised the vital and pivotal contribution of social interaction to cognitive development and the view that cognitive development is a process of continuous interplay between the individual and the environment. It therefore follows that classroom groupings for teaching and peer relationships could have a significant impact on learning.

Finally, it is important for teachers and other professionals in applied learning situations to recognise and foster the possible

Facilitating applied learning

mechanisms for improved learning behaviour (Hertz-Lazarowitz & Miller, 1992). A lack of appropriate social and inter-personal skills can damage opportunities for learner growth and future success, so it is necessary for the teacher to enhance positive learning behaviours in the classroom by encouraging:

- feelings of self-worth;
- a robust sense of self;
- self-reliance;
- autonomy and independence;
- a positive view of the world;
- a sense of personal power.

Taken together, all of these factors successfully considered and implemented will maximise the benefit felt by learners during applied learning experiences.

The teacher–learner relationship and applied learning

Fundamental to the concept of inclusive education is the nature of teacher–learner relationship. Every teacher and every learner is unique, but each shares a common experience through their connection in education.

The 'teacher as role model' can be an underestimated element in effective teaching and learning. It does not mean that the teacher (as in the behaviourist model discussed in Chapter 2) takes control of the classroom and presents themselves to the learners as the font of all knowledge. Rather it should mean that the teacher models appropriate behaviour on how to learn. In an applied learning activity this would mean that the teacher shares their thoughts about the aims and objectives of the task with their learners; the learners are supported in having an opportunity to amend the aims and task to best engage with the learning objective. Teachers can also a model a problem-solving approach for learners, which allows them to see and understand that

Facilitating applied learning

everyone, no matter how experienced, needs to think on their feet, reassess what they already know and apply this in practice.

Professional reflection

If a learner challenges you in the classroom, for example, about your explanation of an activity, you may feel yourself becoming upset or angry. Model good practice to support your learners in developing their own enhanced inter-personal skills. Rather than getting annoyed with the learner, be honest about your feelings and consider why the learner challenged you. You may respond with something like *'Your challenge felt a little inappropriate and made me feel frustrated at first. However, having thought about what I asked you to do, I realise that I could have been clearer and I expect others are also finding the activity hard to complete. (Directed to the class) Will it help if I write instructions for the activity on the board? I want to be sure that everyone in the class is clear and agreed on what we are doing. Thank you for pointing this out to me.'*

How could you maximise the relationship between you and your learners? How could you develop these relationships to facilitate effective applied learning?

Self-awareness and emotional intelligence (Golman, 1995) is a skill that teachers need to cultivate and model. Sharing how to deal with emotive situations, for example, calmly or with humour, can be useful when made explicit to learners as a positive learning experience applied to real classroom situations.

As Golman (1995) observes, the way a teacher behaves 'is in itself a model, a de facto lesson in emotional competence – or lack of thereof'. As learners get older they need to be moving from dependence to independence through increased self-management and responsibility. The teacher needs to foster a teacher–learner relationship that encourages a productive dialogue between them, engaging the learner fully and responsibly in their own learning experience.

Facilitating applied learning

Increasing aspiration and access: The route to higher achievement

Facilitating applied learning is rooted in a belief that teachers have high aspirations for their learners and that all learners have a right to access learning opportunities.

Aspiration relates to having high expectations about what learners can achieve. It reflects a 'can do' mentality displayed when a learner decides to meet challenges and gain access to learning, thus believing that they can succeed. Access means that all learners can benefit from rich and meaningful learning opportunities.

Learners identified with SEND and others vulnerable to underachievement may reduce their aspirations and consequently become demotivated. Learners with low aspirations do not always hold their future in high regard and may not have a vision for Further Education, higher education or extra-curricular activities.

A learner's mindset can greatly affect their desire to access school, college or university to achieve and improve their future. Learners can be disengaged or negative for a number of reasons, ranging from established family views about education to their previous experiences in school. Parental engagement has a very distinct and wide-reaching effect on learner aspirations (Ovenden-Hope & Passy, 2015).

Parents often unintentionally pass their beliefs and feelings on to their children. Furthermore, parents who do not understand the education system may struggle to communicate aspirations to their children. Without good modelling of an aspirational outlook, it can be difficult for children to have their own expectations for education. It is important that learners with SEND and others vulnerable to underachievement feel motivated, not only to overcome potential barriers to learning, but so that they continue to have aspirations about what they are able to achieve. In order for learners to become aspirational in the school environment or to continue to raise their aspirations,

Facilitating applied learning

it is crucial for teachers to be aspirational for all learners and to provide access to a wide range of educational opportunities. Without a whole-school or college culture (which is shared with other settings, such as workplace settings) that models aspirational values and holds a strong belief in the learners' abilities to access and achieve, it is difficult for learners to make the most of their potential.

Learner mindset

Being in the right frame of mind to work independently, actively and creatively may be the greatest hurdle that learners face, particularly if making informed choices and decisions is unfamiliar to them.

The work of Dweck (2006) explores the impact of a fixed and growth mindset and the positive impact of praising a learner's struggle and effort. Dweck suggests that learners' confidence is related to their conception of learning. This is turn produces certain patterns of behaviour when approaching new challenges. Dweck refers to these as 'mastery-oriented' and 'helpless-oriented' behaviours. In applied learning, we aim to engage and develop creative 'mastery-orientated' teaching and learning behaviours.

Young people who display a *mastery* orientation towards a difficult task remain confident in attitude and approach, whereas those who display a helpless-orientation lose focus and concentration and adopt an attitude of failure. Dweck (2000, pp. 7–10) highlighted the following characteristics of mastery-oriented learners and helpless-oriented learners:

Mastery-oriented learners tend to:

- not see themselves as failing;
- engage in self-motivating strategies;
- engage in self-instruction or self-monitoring;
- remain confident that they will succeed;
- have an attitude that they could learn from their failures;
- not see failure as an indictment of themselves as people.

Facilitating applied learning

Case study

The Achievement for All programme has supported leaders and teachers and other staff in raising aspirations across the school (see http://afaeducation.org/ for further information).

By increasing learner confidence through various initiatives, teachers and leaders have worked to change mindsets and attitudes. Parents' aspirations have been raised by sharing their children's achievements and having structured conversations with schools, which allow them to become fully involved in helping their children through education.

The stigma often associated with SEND can be reduced by focusing on whole-school aspirations, so that teachers and leaders become part of and encourage a culture in which all can achieve and progress by setting aspirational targets and having high expectations. By raising learner, parent and teacher aspirations, schools can also help learners to access opportunities and begin to encourage them to focus on specific areas, such as classroom behaviour, attendance and extra-curricular activities, in order to help learners gain access to education and feel part of an inclusive culture.

The innovative Achievement for All framework enables schools to help break down barriers that often prevent children and young people with SEND, and others vulnerable to underachievement, from accessing all the opportunities school has to offer. Many schools have found that the Achievement for All programme has allowed them to improve the access these learners have to the curriculum – leading to increased enjoyment, greater aspiration and higher levels of achievement.

Just as importantly, it has enabled learners to access extra-curricular activities through which they develop positive relationships and enjoy increased participation in school life.

Facilitating applied learning

The helpless-oriented learners tend to:

- quickly denigrate their abilities;
- lose faith in their ability to succeed;
- focus on their failures rather than their successes;
- lose focus on the task;
- abandon strategies they had previously used successfully;
- give up trying more quickly than the mastery-oriented children.

Teachers should be able to tell very quickly once a task is established what type of mindset learners have by the way they engage with the learning. However, if the teacher has assessed their learners' prior learning at the start of their learning journey together, then they will have a good idea of their learners' mindsets and personalised learning needs already.

Collaborative learning

Managing effective collaborative learning is an important skill that any teacher needs to master. A learners' ability to function within a group or team is crucial because of the advantages learning from each other brings and the necessity to relate to and work with others in society and employment (see Chapter 4 on team-work). Roles need to be defined and individuals need to be able to take responsibility for their part in a collaborative task.

Individual contributions to collaborative learning need to be accredited and observed. Learners who do not take responsibility for their own learning need to be monitored and counselled. This requires the teacher to undertake formative assessment throughout a task that uses collaborative learning. It can be done by circulating and observing, giving and recording feedback and asking open questions that probe understanding.

Effective learner participation in group work requires specific objective-oriented accountable roles that are clear to, and hope-

Facilitating applied learning

fully negotiated by, the learners from the outset. By managing and facilitating the collaborative learning experience effectively the teacher will ensure that learners are engaged and motivated and achieve success in terms of both outcome and process (transferable skills developed).

Being open with your learners about the variety of learning experiences available to them will only support them in developing growth mindsets as learners. Knowledge about how to learn establishes the importance of learner voice, not just as a learner council member or in a learning review, but as part of an ongoing dialogue with teachers and peers inspired and informed by all elements of their learning.

Problem-based learning

Problem-based learning (PBL) is a learner-centred approach to learning that encourages learners to work collaboratively to solve problems and to reflect on their experiences. PBL was developed with the rationale that it would 'move students towards the acquisition of knowledge and skills' (Boud & Feletti, 1991) through a structured set of contextualised problems facilitated by relevant resources and teaching support.

Learners are expected to want to learn how to negotiate complex problems through a variety of learning strategies leading to an understanding of the views and concepts involved, an ability to apply this understanding to different situations and thereby realise how competing resolutions can inform decision making.

The typical elements of PBL are as follows:

1   Learners learn by undertaking challenging and open-ended problems.

2   The learning is linked to simulated work-related issues.

3   Learners tend to work in collaborative groups.

4   Teachers are the facilitators of learning, supporting learners in accessing necessary resources and learning materials.

Facilitating applied learning

PBL can be enhanced by imaginative and innovative approaches to the structure of teaching and learning, for example, by using elements of the 'flipped classroom' approach.

Case study: The 'flipped classroom'

The 'flipped classroom' is a way of organising learning that challenges the traditional split between learning that takes place in class and learning that takes place in the learner's own time and space. Learners are expected to engage with directed learning independently and in readiness for developing what they have learned in the classroom with the teacher and their peers. Learning responsibility is 'flipped' from teacher to learner.

The flipped classroom approach makes the most of the flexibility offered by digital technologies to move 'teaching' out of classrooms and into out-of-school settings using video, podcasts or online resources. This means that the classroom becomes the space where time can be 'spent on activities that exercise critical thinking, with the teacher guiding students in creative exploration of the topics they are studying' (Sharples, 2014, p. 4).

Flipped learning, Sharples (2014) argues, makes the classroom a space where 'new approaches to learning and assessment are put into practice' (p. 4). This can include the development of learning and assessment as part of an applied learning approach and/or PBL.

Research on flipped learning is an emerging field, but early findings suggest that the approach can be effective in developing learners' independent and problem-solving skills. For example, Herreid and Schiller (2013) argue that the flipped classroom 'offers us a new model for case study teaching, combining active, student-centered learning with content mastery that can be applied to solving real-world problems. It's a win-win' (p. 65).

In a further illustration of the power of the flipped classroom, Sir Ken Robinson (Robinson & Aronica, 2015) draws on the example of Salman Khan, described as one of the key 'inspirations' for the flipped classroom approach.

Facilitating applied learning

Khan was a successful hedge-fund manager who initially began considering pedagogy when he began tutoring at a distance some younger relatives in their study of mathematics. In 2006, it was suggested to Khan that he use online video technologies to 'scale up' (Robinson & Aronica, 2015, p. 113) his tutoring activities. By 2009, the online 'Khan Academy' had more than 60,000 users.

In mid-2016, the Khan Academy has well over 7 million regular visitors, is supported by Bill Gates and Google, is working directly with 12 schools in the USA and is showing early, but extremely positive, signs that 'the use of Khan Academy may have the potential to improve important. . . student outcomes, including attitudes and motivation toward math and taking responsibility for learning' (Murphy, 2014, p. 43)

Professionalism in practice and professional reflection

A checklist for preparing a problem-based learning (PBL) task:

1 What is the learning objective? (What do I need the learners to learn to achieve programme goals? What do the learners want to learn?)
   For example: Design a mask for a theatre production.

2 Is the 'problem' going to engage all learners? (Should the problem be negotiated with the learners prior to the task being finalised? Will the learners collaborate effectively when researching the problem? Will one task fit all?)
   For example: As a researcher for a mask maker, what would be an appropriate influence for the design and construction of masks for a Greek play set within a play with an overall English Victorian Gothic setting?

3 Does the problem require learners to find and use appropriate knowledge/information/resources? (What will learner achievement criteria look like?)

Facilitating applied learning

> *For example: Learners will need to research at least two historical periods and the design and construction of masks of those times.*
>
> 4 Have I provided or sign-posted where to find this knowledge?
> *For example: Learners might need web links and library resources for extension work and some materials for the classroom.*
>
> 5 Is the timescale realistic to acquire and use the knowledge? How will this knowledge be shared?
> *For example: Learners upload their research into a shared area and role play designers in a peer assessment exercise asking for more information or clarity where needed.*
>
> Now prepare a PBL checklist for a task you will teach this academic year.
> How would you plan for an applied learning PBL activity?
> Who would you need to be included in this process?
> Where would you look for further support?

Functional skills

What are functional skills?

The concept of functional skills was created to support the development of skills necessary for individuals to function in a working environment. 'Functional skills' has become a loaded term, but remains consistent as a requirement for developing learning that is useful for employment.

Functional skills consist of three practical skill areas in: English (sometimes referred to as literacy); information and communication technology (ICT); and mathematics (sometimes referred to as numeracy). Functional skills are taught using applied learning approaches that allow learners to work confidently, effectively and independently in all aspects of their life.

Facilitating applied learning

Functional skills have also been developed into stand-alone units and qualifications at a range of levels to support the individual needs of learners. Functional skills were developed in response to employer requests for an educated workforce that can compete in an increasingly competitive working environment.

How should we teach functional skills?

Learners often have difficulty transferring knowledge, understanding and skills from one area of the curriculum to another and then transferring these into a real-world context. Literacy and numeracy skills are often confined to English and/or mathematics lessons. Employers have highlighted a lack of skills in these basic areas in young employees, despite those employees having relevant qualifications in maths and English. There is an expectation that teachers integrate opportunities for developing learners' abilities in maths and English in all subjects and this can be seen in best practice lesson and programme planning.

Functional skills need to be taught with the employer needs in mind, which requires creativity and subtlety in teaching. This is best done when planning a scheme of work for the whole course, mapping out functional skills development where appropriate.

Teachers may be asked to deliver functional skills in a discrete lesson or integrated into a course or perhaps even across the curriculum with colleagues. This provides an opportunity to use applied learning strategies, to work creatively to engage learners and make the most of the opportunities offered by the settings and knowledge of your partner employers. Remember that functional skills can be taught in a variety of scenarios, from hairdressing to physics, and in settings from newspaper offices to warehouses.

Whatever the circumstance associated with the teaching of functional skills, the importance of highlighting to the learner the particular skill they have learned and how to apply it creatively in other contexts is fundamental to success.

Facilitating applied learning

Professionalism in practice

When you are teaching functional skills, make time to plan lessons and activities with other teachers who teach on the course.

By working together you will ensure that the learners receive a consistent message about the value of functional skills. Collaboration will also ensure that activities are planned to maximise applied learning opportunities.

A case study example of practice

A highly successful applied learning project undertaken by learners at Lenzie Academy provides a clear example from which to develop practice. Lenzie Academy is a comprehensive secondary school with approximately 1,400 pupils and is located in Lenzie, East Dunbartonshire.

The school partners with a local business: A.G. Barr, a major soft drink manufacturer.

A.G. Barr offers an annual competitive challenge to pupils to prepare a business plan, including full costings and resource analysis, to provide a healthy and cost-effective meal for the workforce at A.G. Barr.

The work is pupil-led and undertaken in groups of at least four pupils.

The project naturally lends itself to interdisciplinary learning where young people work across different departments and learn the art of presenting to an audience. Through effective partnership working, the young people and the school benefit from additional expertise and information about the day-to-day running of a business, the workplace and social environment, which enables effective, relevant and contextualised approaches to learning and teaching to take place.

The food and drink industry is also one of Scotland's major employers, and it is therefore important that young people are made aware of the opportunities for training, further study or employment within the industry.

Facilitating applied learning

Health and safety for applied learning

Applied learning should at some point involve applying and developing learning in another setting away from the school, college or university campus. It will also involve working with other adults in the community and employment. It is therefore essential that you follow all safeguarding procedures to ensure that learners are not exposed to any personal risks.

Health and safety and safeguarding relates not only to the people with whom the learners will have contact, but also to the physical environment in which the learning or training takes place, such as regulations on the ratio of adults to learners.

The Disclosure and Barring Service (DBS) helps employers make safer staff recruitment decisions and prevent unsuitable people from working with vulnerable groups, including children. The DBS replaced the Criminal Records Bureau (CRB) and Independent Safeguarding Authority (ISA).

Most schools, colleges and universities will have a department that ensures all safeguarding policies have been followed in relation to work experience, work-based learning or work-related learning. It is always worth the teacher double checking that safeguarding protocols are in place for their learners. The education institution will also need to follow all the guidelines and risk assessment completions for health and safety, which might include (but may not be limited to) trips, visits and offsite work experience and placements.

Professionalism in practice

Identify and ensure that that you are familiar with the following:

- Your school's, college's or university's Health and Safety Policy.
- Your school's, college's or university's Work-based Learning, Work Experience or Offsite Learning Policy.
- Current DBS and safeguarding policy and guidelines.

Facilitating applied learning

Summary

To effectively implement applied learning, teachers must be aware of the factors that can support and challenge their day-to-day practice. These factors may be:

- related to the teacher (such as the teacher's understanding of their own practice, whether that practice is truly inclusive, or whether they have developed good relationships with their learners);

- related to the learner (such as whether the learner has been supported to develop high aspirations of their own potential, or whether the learner has been supported to develop a positive mindset for learning); or

- related to the approach employed (such as teaching strategies that encourage and facilitate collaborative and exploratory learning, or ensuring that the health and safety of all learners are safeguarded in every episode of applied learning).

In the following chapter, we will examine the concept of creativity and why it is fundamental to effective applied learning.

References

Allan, J. (2003). Productive pedagogies and the challenge of inclusion. *British Journal of Special Education, 30*(4), 175–179.

Ben-Ari, R., & Shafir, D. (1988). *Social Integration in Elementary Schools.* Ramat-Gan, Israel: Institute for the Advancement of Social Integration in Schools, Bar-Ilan University.

Booth, T., & Ainscow, M. (2011). *Index for Inclusion: Developing Learning and Participation in Schools.* Bristol: CSIE.

Boud, D., & Feletti, G. (1991). *The Challenge of Problem Based Learning.* London: Kogan Page.

Castelikns, J. (1996). Responsive instruction for young children: A study of how teachers can help easily distracted children become more attentive. *Emotional and Behavioural Difficulties, 1*(1), 22–33.

Centre for Studies on Inclusive Education. (2015). What is inclusive education? Retrieved from www.csie.org.uk/inclusion/what.shtml

Cline, T. (1992). *The Assessment of Special Educational Needs.* London: Paul Chapman Publishing.

Facilitating applied learning

Cornwall, J., & Tod, J. (1998). *IEPS: Emotional and Behavioural Difficulties*. London: David Fulton.

Dweck, C. (2000). *Self-Theories: Their Role in Motivation, Personality and Development*. Hove, East Sussex: Psychology Press.

Dweck, C. (2006). *Mindset*. New York: Random House.

Education Scotland. (n.d.). Entrepreneurial skills – Lenzie Academy. Retrieved from Education Scotland: www.educationscotland.gov.uk/resources/practice/e/lenzie/nextsteps.asp?strReferringChannel=learningandteaching&strReferringPageID=tcm:4-616171-64

Fröbel, F. (1826). *On the Education of Man (Die Menschenerziehung)*. Keilhau/Leipzig: Wienbrach.

Golman, D. (1995). *Emotional Intelligence: Why It Can Matter More than IQ*. New York: Bantam Books.

Herreid, C. F., & Schiller, N. A. (2013). Case study: Case studies and the Flipped Classroom. *Journal of College Science Teaching, 42*(5), 62–67.

Hertz-Lazarowitz, R., & Miller, N. (1992). *Interaction in Cooperative Groups*. New York: Cambridge University Press.

Moll, L. C., & Whitmore, K. F. (1998). Vykotsky in classroom practice: Moving from individual transmission to social transaction. In D. Faulkner, K. Littleton, & M. Woodhead, *Learning Relationships in the Classroom*. London: Routledge.

Montessori, M. (1966). *The Human Tendencies and Montessori Education*. Amsterdam: Association Montessori Internationale.

Munby, S. (1994). Assessment and pastoral care: Sense, sensitivity and standards. In R. Best, P. Lang, C. Lodge, & C. Watkins, *Pastoral Care and Personal – Social Education: Entitlement and Provision*. London: Cassell.

Murphy, R. (2014). *Research on the Use of Khan Academy in Schools*. Menlo Park, CA: SRI International.

OECD. (2005). *Teachers Matter – Attracting, Developing and Retaining Effective Teachers*. Paris: OECD.

Ovenden-Hope, T., & Passy, R. (2015). Changing cultures in coastal academies. Cornwall: Plymouth University, The Cornwall College Group. Retrieved 1 April 2015, from www.cornwall.ac.uk/sites/default/files/documents/Coastal%20Academies%20Report_2015_final_2%20Tanya%20Ovenden-Hope%20and%20Rowena%20Passy.pdf

Piaget, J. (1951). *The Psychology of Intelligence*. London: Routledge and Kegan Paul.

Prawat, R. S., & Nickerson, J. R. (1985). The relationship between teacher thought and action and student affective outcomes. *The Elementary School Journal, 85*(4), 529–540.

Robinson, K., & Aronica, L. (2015). *Creative Schools: Revolutionizing Education from the Ground Up*. London: Allen House.

Serrow, R. C., & Salomon, D. (1979). Classroom climates and students' intergroup behaviour. *Journal of Educational Psychology, 71*(5), 669–676.

Sharples, M. (2014). *Innovating Pedagogy 2014: Open University Innovation Report 3*. Milton Keynes: The Open University.

Facilitating applied learning

Stainback, S., Stainback, W., Esat, K., & Sapon-Shevin, M. (1994). A commentary on inclusion and the development of a positive self-identity by people with disabilities. *Exceptional Children, 60*(6), 486–490.

Stoll, L., Fink, D., & Earl, L. (2003). *It's About Learning (and it's About Time): What's in it for Schools?* London: Routledge Falmer.

Vygotsky, L. S. (1962). *Thought and Language* (E. Hanfmann, & G. Vakar, Eds.). Cambridge, MA: MIT Press.

CHAPTER 6

Creativity in applied learning

This chapter will:

- explain why the concept of creativity is important to applied learning;
- discuss how teachers can develop creativity in learners;
- describe some creative approaches to teaching;
- suggest some topics for professional reflection.

Why is creativity important?

It is very difficult to predict – especially the future.
– Commonly attributed to Neils Bohr (Danish physicist)

Our global economy revolves around a world of digital technology, interaction with which requires creative thinking for learning and development in this area. Yet external measures of institutional educational performance can limit meaningful risk-taking strategies for learning, strategies that could promote and enhance creativity.

Creativity in applied learning

In our everyday lives we will have contact with cars. Cars are maintained by mechanics and verified as roadworthy through the MOT process. The MOT process involves the use of technology more complex than that which was required to put a human on the moon! This everyday, commonplace activity has emerged through creative thinking for innovative development. Emergency services officers use digital communications to save lives by being in constant and real-time contact with colleagues and experts who support those who require help. Teachers and other professionals use digital tools to maximise the engagement of learners, as well as to track the progress of learners over time and subject areas.

These technological innovations required creativity from their inventors, but it is important to remember that they increasingly require creativity from their users to make the most of the innovations' application to benefit the user's life. This requirement for creativity will only increase as young people today move into their future lives.

It is important for us to remember that the skills, competencies and knowledge required by young people today will be much more difficult for us to predict than it was to predict the world of today from the twentieth century. However, what is certain is that developing these skills, competencies and knowledges will include maximising learners' creative skills and putting in place 'creative teaching' in applied learning.

This is not a view that will be new to many teachers. In his 2006 online TED Talk 'Do schools kill creativity?' (which has been viewed nearly 35 million times), Sir Ken Robinson reflected on how challenging it is for education to prepare learners for the future:

> I have a big interest in education, and I think we all do. We have a huge vested interest in it, partly because it's education that's meant to take us into this future that we can't grasp. If you think of it, children starting school this year will be retiring in 2065. Nobody has a clue [. . .] what the world will

108

Creativity in applied learning

look like in five years' time. And yet we're meant to be educating them for it. So the unpredictability, I think, is extraordinary.

(Robinson, 2006)

Many thinkers from fields other than education have highlighted the concept of 'creativity' as a key ingredient in the development of learning and comprehension skills in any context. For example, Taleb (2007) identifies creative, innovative and self-regulated learning as a key factor in the early rise of clinical science and the parallel decline in 'medieval medicine'. Similarly, the Italian semiotician Umberto Eco wrote extensively on the creative skills demanded from the 'model reader' when decoding or interpreting any text for any reason, noting that this is the case for 'Finnegan's Wake but also for a railway timetable' (Eco, 1995, p. 27).

In line with this, contemporary research underlines the crucial importance of developing skills and competencies for learners who will become adults in the middle of the twenty-first century. For example, the high-profile Microsoft Partners in Learning/ITL Research project '21st Century Learning Design' (Microsoft Educator Network, n.d.) has identified six 'rubrics' of twenty-first century learning, each of which represents 'an important skill for students to develop':

- collaboration;
- knowledge construction;
- self-regulation;
- real-world problem-solving and innovation;
- the use of ICT for learning;
- skilled communication.

In line with these findings, as we have discussed in Chapter 1, the 2016 CBI/Pearson report (CBI, 2016) notes that businesses and employers today are looking for two key capacities in young people: 'key skills and knowledge' such as 'literacy/use of English

Creativity in applied learning

. . . and basic numeracy' and also 'skills that go beyond academic ability (such as communication skills, problem solving skills, analysis skills, resilience, and creativity' (pp. 31–32), which 'are essential skills for the workplace and the rest of life' (p. 32).

The obvious economic need for learners to develop transferable skills sits counterintuitively with the policy and processes that govern education curriculum and assessment, such as the return to knowledge-based synoptic examinations. To counter commonly held assumptions that an externally assessed curriculum cannot support creativity in the classroom, we will now consider how teachers might embed creative thinking into learning experiences and the benefits this approach may bring to the learner.

Creativity in applied learning

Embedding creativity and creative thinking into the learning experience of young people may seem daunting to already busy teachers, but in terms of successful learner engagement and motivation it is, in most cases, more than worth the effort.

Creative expression and creative thinking are often confused in educational terms and therefore some clarification will help to distinguish between them in planning creativity into applied learning experiences.

Creative expression is linked to the arts and is a form of artistic interpretation and self-expression. Creative expression is of course present in some learning outcomes in subjects from literature to hairdressing, car design to marketing, but it may not develop into innovative new ways of doing.

Creative thinking allows a way of finding new and innovative solutions to problems and challenges. Creative thinking could be new to the learner, such as working out how to build a strong bridge from spaghetti, or new to the world and therefore of historical and social significance, such as Einstein's theory of relativity.

110

Creativity in applied learning

Professional reflection

You may have questioned the wisdom of building bridges with spaghetti in the paragraph above, but in terms of a teaching strategy it might encourage you to think laterally and use your own creative thinking for planning learning experiences that are not only REAL but may lead to the next Einstein!

Case study: Visible Media

The 2008 report 'Creative Opportunities' commissioned by the National Endowment for Science, Technology and the Arts (Nesta, 2008) includes a case study of applied learning carried out in partnership between schools in Newcastle-Upon-Tyne and Visible Media.

Visible Media is a 'small enterprise producing video, photography and multimedia products for a range of clients in both the private and public sectors' (p. 48).

Every year six school students aged 14–18 are given the opportunity to gain a week's work experience at the company. The learners participate in 'all aspects of the creative business, including meeting clients, working on projects and using up-to-date digital technology including software such as Photoshop and digital video editing packages' (p. 49).

The learners who participate 'gain "hard", "sub sector-specific" skills in areas such as video, multimedia and design. They also learn wider skills that are vital for employability' (p. 49).

The authors of the report observe that schools also gain from the experience through 'a hands on aspect to the vocational and work-related learning offered to their students' (p. 49).

The authors conclude that:

> The work experience at Visible Media includes mentoring from the staff of the company and peer

111

Creativity in applied learning

> mentoring between the student pairs who participate. The entrepreneur behind the scheme takes a mentoring role as she goes out into the educational community to pass on her knowledge and experience. Mentoring is a vital element of professional development, and creative entrepreneur mentors are invaluable in influencing young people in their own creative entrepreneurial aspirations. [. . .] The work experience programme at Visible Media provides examples of best practice that could be replicated, and lessons that could be learned for those involved in or interested in becoming involved in providing and accessing work-related learning with creative SMEs.
>
> (pp. 49–50)
>
> Full details can be found at the NESTA website, at:
> www.nesta.org.uk/publications/creative-opportunities

Creativity, in an educational setting, is developed when learners are actively involved in their own learning. Scaffolding learning can provide a valuable tool for enabling learners to develop creativity and creative thinking.

Scaffolding involves supporting the learner to help them build on previous knowledge and learn new information, in order to achieve the intended outcome of the activity. The teacher provides support that is literally scaffolding – the structure around the experience that allows learners to build their own understanding. The scaffolding structure is built by the teacher through questioning, prompting, pointing things out and modelling learning behaviours and approaches.

Crucially, as is the case with the scaffolding we see on buildings, the technique also includes dismantling or 'fading' the support as each achievement is realised, independence sought and confidence gained.

Creativity in applied learning

Case study: Faking it . . . as a published poet

The ICE (Innovation, Creativity and Enterprise) House Project (Cornwall College and Plymouth University) was funded by the European Social Fund with an aim to develop innovation creativity and enterprising behaviours in learners through teacher training that prepared teachers to facilitate ICE.

Using ideas developed with trainee teachers, the ICE House team supported applied learning in a non-work related context through an authentic creative challenge in a school. The learning objective was to raise learner attainment in speaking and listening through the analysis of poetry. The initial challenge for the teacher was to find a context and an authentic challenge for poetry analysis to make it more meaningful and engaging to the learners.

In their curriculum time learners were challenged to produce their own poetry that was of a sufficiently high standard so as not to draw attention to it when presented and analysed alongside the work of published poets. The learners composed and analysed their poetry and then consulted a poet about what they had written.

The learners then planned an event with an adult panel in which they attempted to meet the challenge set. The learners were encouraged to take responsibility for the challenge and work in an independent and adult way, co-constructing and directing much of the project.

They planned and delivered poetry lessons and coordinated teacher-led sessions in the run up to the event. They decided on the 'speed dating' and a questionnaire assessment approach for the presentation of the poetry.

The learners involved in 'Faking it' were also observed in an unrelated whole-year activity day, and were seen to be able to transfer the skills developed through the poetry challenge into leading and organising collaborative learning on the activity day. So obvious was the development of their skill base it is was remarked upon by other teachers who had not been involved in the challenge.

The 'faking it' case study is an example of an authentic creative learning challenge; the essence of applied learning. It was REAL – relevant, engaged active learning.

Creativity in applied learning

Professional reflection

Thinking about the 'Faking it' case study, how could you develop your practice to include creative authentic challenges for your learners?

How might this inform your approach to supporting learners to develop a mastery oriented attitude and approach to learning?

The creative teacher as researcher

Truly creative teaching requires a teacher to understand what works in teaching and why, and to use this understanding to develop new ways of thinking about and doing teaching. A most effective way for a teacher to be creative and independent in their own professional development is to use evidence to inform practice. To facilitate this engagement a teacher must become an effective educational researcher, seeking credible sources of evidence from which to develop pedagogy (teenagogy) and practice.

Educational policy in England and teacher engagement is driving an evidence-based and research-informed teaching profession, with teachers taking research methods learned in their higher qualifications and initial teacher training to help them find creative solutions to challenges in their practice. ResearchED (www.workingoutwhatworks.com) is a great example of teachers from across the globe coming together to share and collaborate on research-informed teaching. ResearchEd has a growing number of events in England for school and college teachers, which have been supported by government policy calling for a more evidence-based approach in teaching (DfE, 2016).

Ben Goldacre's 2013 report to the Department for Education highlighted the need for a culture in schools where best practice is used as a 'matter of routine' (Goldacre, 2013). Researching an area of practice is an inherently creative act. Top performing

Creativity in applied learning

educational systems, for example, in Singapore, encourage teachers to base their practice on their own evidence-based research.

Action research

Action research is a form of self-reflective inquiry undertaken by participants in social situations in order to improve their own practices, as well as their understanding of those practices, and the situations in which the practices are carried out. In education, action research is when a teacher undertakes research into their teaching activity, this could be to help identify a solution to an issue, or provide a means of developing an area of practice.

Action research can also provide an appropriate way forward for managing change or developing institutional improvement in an educational setting. Action research involves the identification of a practical problem or issue, which is then changed through individual or collaborative intervention. It is then analysed and evaluated. The problem(s) may not be clearly defined and the change process may evolve through the process.

The action research process

Aim: An overall statement of what the research wants to achieve/explore/find out.

Research questions: A short set of focused questions or statements that guide the area for investigation.

Literature review: The related evidence base of existing knowledge in the area you are investigating. What research has already been carried out in the area? Who are the key researchers/theorists in this area? This should be a systematic outline of key research (use key related words for searches and keep a note of the words you have used). If it is a desk-based literature review, have you covered all possible areas (national and international databases)?

115

Creativity in applied learning

Method: How you will go about finding the answers to your research question/s. Who will you 'speak' to? How will you 'speak' to them to collect data? Questionnaires? Interviews? What secondary data will you look at? How many people will be investigated? (it is important to look at the size of the sample and consider if this is appropriate) Do you want your findings to be generalisable to other schools or colleges? Does your methodology support this?

Findings: The results of your investigations, or what you found out.

Conclusions: Findings analysed in relation to your research questions. You will provide a discussion of what you believe you can infer from the results.

Recommendations: Your conclusions may support recommendations for policy or practice.

Published reports usually have an executive summary: Summarise the overall research aim, research questions (objectives), method, findings, conclusion and recommendations. Provide an overall picture for easy access to your research.

Professional reflection and professionalism in practice

Consider your classroom practice and reflect on an area you would like to know more about, or would like to do differently, or would like to change.

Write an action research plan based on the process above for your area of inquiry.

You may find it helpful to google key words for your area of inquiry linked to research, e.g. 'recent research white, working-class attainment gap England', and look at some reports as examples of what and how to start your investigation. You may find when you read these reports that you do not agree with their conclusions based on your own experiences. This is a great stimulus for becoming an action researcher. If you do not agree with other researchers' findings, conduct your own research. Have

116

Creativity in applied learning

confidence in what you know about teaching and learning; after all, you are a professional and 'live in your lab' every working day. Disseminate your findings to other teachers and educational researchers, so that your professional community can benefit from what you have learned.

The British Educational Research Association (BERA) is actively encouraging teachers to become members and participate in events and activities that disseminate and discuss educational research findings. For more information see www.bera.ac.uk.

Summary

Creativity is a key concept when we consider the needs of today's learners as adults in the twenty-first century. Teachers need to support learners in developing a wide range of creative thinking skills (such as problem-solving and research skills), and employ creative teaching approaches.

Applied learning is an approach that can meet both of these creativity needs, but requires teachers to expand their thinking and assumptions beyond 'traditional' concepts of teaching and learning.

In the following chapter, we will examine how reflective learning can support teachers and educators to challenge their assumptions and develop their knowledge, understanding and practice as education professionals.

References

CBI. (2016). *The Right Combination – The CBI/Pearson Education and Skills Survey 2016*. London: Pearson.

DfE. (2016). *Educational Excellence Everywhere*. London: DfE.

Eco, U. (1995). *Six Walks in the Fictional Woods*. Cambridge, MA: Harvard University Press.

Goldacre, B. (2013). *Building Evidence into Education*. London: DfE.

Microsoft Educator Network. (n.d.). Retrieved from https://education.microsoft.com/GetTrained/ITL-Research

Creativity in applied learning

Nesta. (2008). Creative opportunities. Retrieved from http://www.nesta.org.uk/publications/creative-opportunities

Robinson, K. (2006, February). Do schools kill creativity? Retrieved from TED: www.ted.com/talks/ken_robinson_says_schools_kill_creativity?language=en

Taleb, N. N. (2007). *The Black Swan*. London: Penguin.

CHAPTER 7

Reflective learning and self-evaluation in practice

This chapter will:

- explain the concept of reflective learning for teachers;
- discuss how professional reflection can develop a teacher's professional practice;
- describe some effective approaches for professional reflection;
- suggest some topics for professional reflection.

To ensure that teaching continues to develop and meet learner needs, it is important to both reflect on and evaluate (consider the strengths and areas for improvement of) practice.

Reflection provides a means of analysing experience and making decisions about future action based on interpretations of processes and outcomes. This chapter will explore reflective learning in practice as a process through which teachers may monitor their actions to inform change for teaching and learning.

119

Reflective learning and self-evaluation in practice

Reflective learning

Schön (1983) talks of reflection-in-action as a process through which professionals constantly monitor their actions and make instantaneous decisions based on their tacit knowledge. He distinguishes this from reflection-on-action, which is a more deliberate analysis, undertaken after the event. Schön suggests that professionals in fields such as education need to reflect on practice situations, because these are not always clear cut and require professional judgement.

To help to extend the process of reflection Brookfield suggests the use of four 'critical lenses' to consider different perspectives on events (Brookfield, 1995). In addition to our own view of events (lens one), he suggests we should consider things from the perspective of our learners (lens two), our colleagues (lens three) and also take into account what our knowledge of theory and research can offer (lens four). This approach to reflection can certainly help teachers move beyond immediate problems identified in practice and open up to wider issues that may be linked to what is being considered.

Reflective learning can be developed by keeping a reflective log or journal in which thoughts about lessons, learner progress etc. are recorded. Sharing thoughts or experiences about practice with colleagues, peers or mentors can provide opportunities to go beyond what can be achieved by reflecting independently (Brockbank & McGill, 1998; Bolton, 2005).

Collaborative reflective learning enables consideration of other viewpoints and interpretations of events, which can offer new insight on how to move forward with an issue or establish that something does not require change. Peer reflections can also feel challenging to any deeply held views and assumptions and may be rejected (Pope, 2005); however, it is important to take time to consider whether others' views are useful in developing greater understanding.

Reflective learning is not always an easy process, but it has tremendous potential for extending teacher development as both

Reflective learning and self-evaluation in practice

practitioner and contributor to wider educational debate. It is the reason why we have included professional reflection prompts throughout this book!

> **Professional reflection**
>
> To what extent are you aware of your engagement with reflection-in-action and reflection-on action in your own practice?
>
> Think of a recent event that prompted you to reflect. Was this 'in-action' while you were teaching or 'on-action' after the lesson? How did you reflect? Was your reflection structured? Did you write your reflections down? Did this reflection lead to improvement in your practice? How, or why not?
>
> Identify clear opportunities in your working week for reflective learning.

Self-evaluation

Self-development is systematic; we never stop learning and developing, and sustained self-evaluation is critical to meaningful development as a teacher.

> People with a high level of personal mastery live in a continual learning mode. They never 'arrive'. People with a high level of personal mastery are acutely aware of their ignorance, their incompetence, their growth areas. And they are deeply self-confident. Paradoxical? Only for those who do not see that the journey is the reward.
>
> (Senge, 1990, p. 142)

By considering how self-evaluation works, this section examines the role of values and beliefs in developing practice. We also consider the extent to which the values and beliefs of the

Reflective learning and self-evaluation in practice

educational setting influence the development of teachers and ultimately the outcomes for learners.

The culture of the teaching profession and the role of the support staff in educational settings are changing, reflecting the changing society in which we live, with its proliferation of cultures, beliefs and values. The school, college or university community work towards a common goal, reaching for and achieving targets. In practice, teachers and other professionals need to understand their actions and behaviours at work in relation to their beliefs and values. If the two do not equate, teachers should consider how this may impact on learner needs.

Schools, colleges, universities – all educational settings – should be places in which success is celebrated. Teachers will willingly participate in the change process of their institution if they agree with its mission and values. Self-evaluation and effective self-development can influence practice in a positive way, supporting teachers in understanding their professional standpoint, competencies and areas for change.

A fundamental issue in teacher development is the ability to recognise where an individual is in relation to where we would like to be:

> Self-evaluation of professional competence is more than an assessment of traditional conformity or technical account-ability. It is assessed in terms of moral and prudent answerability for practical judgements actually made within the context of existing educational institutions.
>
> (Carr & Kemmis, 1986, p. 31)

As a process, self-evaluation should inform our day-to-day professional practice. An effective teacher will be honest and open in their evaluation of their practice. Self-evaluation involves making sense of our contribution in situations that involve team-work, professional knowledge and understanding, professional relationships and preparation for teaching (see Table 7.1).

Reflective learning and self-evaluation in practice

Professional reflection

Practitioner self-evaluation questions:

- What do I value?
- What is my present professional situation?
- Where would I like my career to lead?
- How might I get there?
- What help is available?

Personal qualities needed:
Do I have . . .

- the ability to self-manage?
- clear personal values?
- clear personal objectives?
- an emphasis on continuing personal growth?
- effective problem-solving skills?
- the capacity to be creative and innovative?

Table 7.1 Self-evaluation situations

Team-work:	Relationships with:
– listening	– parents
– attitude	– colleagues
– flexibility	– children
Knowledge and understanding of:	**Preparation of:**
– current publications	– lessons
– equal opportunity issues	– monitoring procedures
– learning styles	– assessment

Professional reflection

Consider each of the four categories in Table 7.1. Reflect on how you could give your 'best performance' as a teacher for each item listed.

Consider how this could impact on outcomes for your learners.

Reflective learning and self-evaluation in practice

A model for self-evaluation

We have considered in the previous section the importance of self-evaluation in improving personal and professional performance and, ultimately, the experiences and outcomes of learners. Now we will take this a step further by looking at a practice-based model for professional self-evaluation.

The model of self-evaluation presented below encourages teachers, and other educational professionals, to examine work practices and related attitudes, identifying what is done well, what could be done better and maybe what should not be done at all. Effective self-evaluation can lead to improved performance, and can also result in a better balance between work and home.

A practice-based approach to self-evaluation is shown in Figure 7.1. In this example the questions are designed to help a teacher, or other education professional, make sense of their role and position in a range of situations.

Any change informed by self-evaluation should be monitored, evaluated and reviewed to ascertain whether the change has improved practice or outcomes for learners.

Professional reflection

Look at Figure 7.1 and ask 'Where am I in this process of self-evaluation?'

You should consider the question in relation to where you are now. Apply your learning by framing your answers on theoretical knowledge or practical experience.

Now reflect on how self-evaluation can support and develop your use of applied learning. A challenge identified for teachers facilitating applied learning has been finding the time to set up relevant, engaged, active learning lessons. Could self-evaluation be the key to establishing the time to invest in applied learning?

124

Reflective learning and self-evaluation in practice

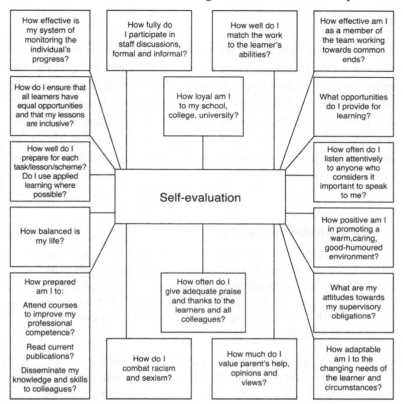

Figure 7.1 A model for self-evaluation

Are things working more effectively or not? It is important to remember that it is often difficult to test the outcome of change against the original objectives; after all, education institutions are dynamic, as are the learners and teachers within them.

Setting clear, measurable objectives at the outset of any change process is essential. It is important to start this process with a projected end point and an identification of what success looks like. The following sections will examine the importance of monitoring, evaluation and review in making positive changes to practice.

Reflective learning and self-evaluation in practice

Monitoring

Following the implementation of a strategy for change, it is important to monitor its progress and outcomes against the objectives set. If the plan is not monitored, it will not be possible to determine whether the objectives have been achieved. Monitoring will also enable the teacher to inform leaders on impact relating to the change, which will support them in informing whole institutional change and available resources to enable this.

Professionalism in practice

Wilson (2004) provides some questions that schools should consider when developing tools or techniques to measure the effectiveness of something they deliver. The questions below have been adapted from Wilson and offer a good framework for monitoring specific changes in applied learning situations:

1 Which outcomes do you wish to measure? (For example, changes in behaviour, or attainment etc.)
2 What baseline evidence will be needed? How can this be obtained? What new systems need to be established? Who will be responsible?
3 What evidence is there of the 'quality' of this change at different times? How does this inform future development?
4 How are the purposes and the results of the evidence collection discussed and shared?
5 How reliable or valid is the evidence that is available?
6 How is the evidence used and how are results analysed to inform learning in the future?
7 How might the skills of staff in using evaluation be developed?
8 How are results used to inform whole setting planning and development?

(Adapted from Wilson, 2004, p. 30)

Reflective learning and self-evaluation in practice

Most significantly, monitoring change will provide a framework in which teachers can reflect on their own practice, an outcome of which is enhanced job satisfaction. Consistent monitoring promotes reflective practice.

Monitoring is an ongoing activity and it is integral to teaching and learning, being based on both *practice* and *outcomes*. Everard, Morris, and Wilson (2004) underline the need for 'yardsticks' by which to recognise when the objectives have been achieved and which can be used 'to set a ratchet to prevent backsliding'. Effective monitoring must also include 'managing the processes needed to take corrective action in case of a shortfall' (Everard et al., 2004, p. 285) that will enable teachers to obtain the best results from the available resources.

Everard et al. (2004) further advocate setting up 'as part of the overall plan for change', strategies for 'gathering reliable information and analysing it . . . in order to measure if the change has been effective and has become truly assimilated' (p. 285).

Evaluation

The value of evaluation, of examining the strengths and weaknesses of something, is well rehearsed as part of effective development. Hall and Oldroyd (1990) suggest that: 'Evaluation is a component of development planning and an essential prerequisite to preparing any subsequent plan.' Everard et al. (2004) suggest that evaluation will highlight any 'unforeseen consequences of the change' that can subsequently be managed or 'made the subject of further change'.

Essentially, evaluation is a collaborative exercise that involves:

- asking questions;
- gathering information;
- forming conclusions;

in order to:

- make recommendations.

Reflective learning and self-evaluation in practice

Professionalism in practice: A checklist for elements of evaluation

1 Identify a clear purpose that includes:
- broad guidelines or aims;
- objectives;
- indicators of desired outcomes.

2 Design questions that are:
- unambiguous;
- penetrating;
- useful;
- relevant.

3 Access information that is:
- accessible;
- meaningful;
- related to questions;
- manageable.

4 Form conclusions that consider:
- educational (institutional and national) conditions;
- obstacles and opportunities;
- effects;
- assumptions;
- alternatives.

5 Deliver reports that are:
- concise;
- informative;
- focused on audience's need;
- able to inform decision making.

6 Write a good evaluation brief:
- that specifies most, if not all, of the above.

(Adapted from Hall & Oldroyd, 1990)

In contrast to monitoring, evaluation encompasses reviewing and analysing the status and progress of a plan's objectives. Through the evaluation process, teachers will determine the need to change objectives, priorities and/or practice. Hargreaves

Reflective learning and self-evaluation in practice

and Hopkins (1991) and Parsons and Burkey (2011) stress the importance of evaluation (both micro and macro) in enhancing the professional judgement of all teachers during any period of change.

The final stage in the evaluation process is to write a report that includes and considers purpose, content, process, context and outcomes. Ultimately any evaluation is undertaken to support understanding of what and/or how something can be changed for the better. Teachers that engage with evaluating their teaching, their learners' learning, their programme etc. will support better practice. The detailed processes of reflective learning, self-evaluation, monitoring and evaluation provided above will open opportunities to consider how, when and why to use applied learning to support better practice.

Summary

Professional reflective learning allows teachers to deeply and rigorously consider their practice, beliefs and assumptions. Embedding these reflections in self-evaluation models and making change as a consequence enables teachers to improve both the opportunities and outcomes for learners.

Reflection, evaluation and change is especially relevant to applied learning. Effective applied learning requires teachers and other professionals to continually 'think outside the box' to react to and meet the changing needs of their learners and the changing world in which they live.

References

Bolton, G. (2005). *Reflective Practice: Writing and Professional Development*. London: Sage.

Brockbank, A., & McGill, I. (1998). *Facilitating Reflective Learning in Higher Education*. Buckingham: SRHE/Open University Press.

Brookfield, S. (1995). *Becoming a Critically Reflective Teacher*. San-Francisco, CA: Jossey-Bass.

Carr, W., & Kemmis, S. (1986). *Becoming Critical: Education, Knowledge and Action Research*. Lewes: Falmer Press.

Reflective learning and self-evaluation in practice

Everard, K. B., Morris, G., & Wilson, I. (2004). *Effective School Management* (4th ed.). London: Paul Chapman Publishing.

Hall, I., & Oldroyd, D. (1990). *Management Self-development for Staff in Secondary Schools, Unit 2: Policy, Planning and Change*. Bristol: NDCEMP.

Hargreaves, D. H., & Hopkins, D. (1991). *The Empowered School: The Management and Practice of Development Planning*. London: Cassell.

Parsons, D., & Burkey, S. (2011). *Evaluation of the Teaching and Learning Research Programme (Second Phase)*. London: ESRC.

Pope, N. (2005). The impact of stress in self- and peer assessment. *Assessment & Evaluation in Higher Education, 30*(1), 51–63.

Schön, D. A. (1983). *The Reflective Practitioner: How Professionals Think in Action*. New York: Basic Books.

Senge, P. M. (1990). *The Fifth Discipline: The Art and Practice of the Learning Organization*. New York: Doubleday/Currency.

Wilson, D. (2004). Which ranking? The impact of a 'value added' measure of secondary school performance. *Public Money and Management, 24*(1), 37–45.

Conclusion

Applied learning involves a complex mix of skills, connections and knowledge that have to be understood by the teacher in order to be facilitated effectively in their teaching. In order for teachers to embrace REAL (Relevant, Engaging, Active Learning) opportunities, they need time to plan, a mindset and approach that champions learner independence and personal need, and an acceptance that authentic experiences develop learners.

Applied learning should be:

- Experiential (provide purpose, direction and application).

- Contextual (relevant to real life, particularly working life).

- Personal (meet the learners' needs).

Applied learning can utilise a variety of teaching and learning strategies, from problem-based learning to authentic creative challenges. Whatever strategies the teachers decide to use, they should provide choice for learners and opportunities for them to co-construct their learning experiences.

Applied learning is at its best when learners can see the connection with working life, so teachers should seek to develop and maintain good links with employers and have an up-to-date

Conclusion

understanding of the relevant skills sectors and employment opportunities linked to the subjects they teach.

Achieving high-quality applied learning is not easy; it takes careful planning to include professionals from the workplace, create real investigations, apply learning to different contexts and establish opportunities for creative thinking and taking on board the learners' choices and needs. However, once a teacher has experienced effective applied learning, they realise that learners' engagement, motivation and development have made all the effort, reflection and evaluation worthwhile.

The case studies for applied learning used in this book are real and have come from teachers who have evaluated the applied learning event/task/project and been able to share the findings and conclusions with other educational professionals. We hope that this book will develop your understanding and practice in applied learning and we look forward to your case studies being shared in the future. Keep it REAL!

Glossary

Andragogy is a term created from the Greek word 'andros' meaning man and 'agogos' meaning leader, but used to refer to the teaching of adults. The term 'andragogy' was originally formulated by a German teacher, Alexander Kapp, in 1833. However, Malcolm Knowles introduced the term (then spelled 'androgogy') in 1968 and developed a theory of adult learning education in 1970.

Applied learning is a strategy used in teaching for developing Relevant, Engaging, Active Learning (REAL). It is relevant due to the use of practical and/or real life situations, e.g. work, to improve understanding of how theory works in practice. It is engaging and active for learners based on lesson and programme planning that embeds creativity, learner-centred tasks and activities, e.g. PBL, team-work, increasing independence and use of transferable skills.

Authentic creative challenge is designed with specific learners in mind to stretch them and develop a creative response with open-ended outcome. It differs from PBL and CPS (see below) in that it has a real-world context and the results have an impact, however small, beyond the classroom. The ideal authentic challenge leads to an improvement for others.

Glossary

Behaviourism focuses on teacher and learner behaviour, with learning occurring as a result of transmission of knowledge by the teacher to the learners (Skinner, 1972; Bandura, 1986). The goal is to achieve exemplary outcomes for learners through expert teacher knowledge and clear 'rewards' (good and bad) for learners as a system of control. For 14–19-year-olds learning would be through more didactic strategies, which ensure that the expert teacher is in control of the learning experience.

Creative problem solving differs from problem-based learning (PBL) (see below) in that the open-ended task requires genuine innovative or original thinking to solve a problem with many possible outcomes and solutions.

Disaffection is the experience of the learner who has lost interest in learning manifested in lack of motivation and lack of engagement or in extreme as disruptive behaviour.

Formative assessment is an evaluation of the learners' learning that aids understanding and development of their knowledge, skills and abilities without making a final or summative judgement on their level of learning. Formative assessment is undertaken through observation, questioning and feedback by the teacher to the learner, or through self and peer assessment.

Humanism values the emotional and developmental needs of the learner above all other things (Rogers, 1969; Maslow, 1943). Learning will occur in an environment of trust, where the teacher acts as facilitator for the learners' own learning needs and ambitions. Fourteen to nineteen year olds are considered eager to learn and should be given responsibility for directing for their own learning, with teachers facilitating this process by listening to their learners' feelings and encouraging the learners to self-evaluate. An interesting example of a humanist approach in compulsory schooling is Summerhill School, an independent British boarding school that was founded in 1921 with the belief that the school should be made to fit the child, rather than the other way around.

Glossary

Metacognition is how an individual understands their mental processes, which includes their understanding of their own learning, and their understanding of how to learn.

Pedagogy derives from the Greek 'paidagogia', 'paid' meaning child and 'agogos' meaning leader. Thus, pedagogy originally meant education, attendance on children. The teacher-centred model has been central to the pedagogical model. The teacher, according to this model, has full responsibility for making decisions about what will be learned, how it will be learned, when it will be learned, and determining if the material has been learned. Pedagogy, therefore, places the learner in a submissive role.

Problem-based learning (PBL) is a strategy where the learners learn through being set a problem that requires them to research and develop a solution within specific parameters. The process of finding a solution and the learning involved is more important than the solution itself.

Social constructivism is a psychological school of thought that describes how learning happens through the process of thought. The theory of constructivism suggests that learners construct knowledge out of their experiences and is often associated with pedagogic approaches that promote active learning or learning by doing. Piaget (1951) and Vygotsky (1931) offered theories that identified stages at which the maturation of the learning would enable more complex types of learning. For the 14–19 age range, learning would be at a 'formal operational level' (Piaget, 1951) of logical hypothesising and learners in the Zone of Proximal Development (ZPD) where maturation of ability to learn independently is well developed for (Vygotsky, 1978). Teachers are facilitators and learners participate actively in constructing meaning about what they are learning.

Teenagogy offers a concept for the teaching of teenagers through strategies that engage and motivate this age range to learn and

Glossary

develop knowledge, skills and behaviours appropriate for success.

Work-related learning links subject matter to the world of work directly and may involve work-based simulations or real-world experience, ranging from employer talks to visits to employment settings.

Index

Note: Page numbers in **bold** refer to tables and page numbers in *italics* refer to figures.

access, of learners 93–5
achievement: aspiration 93–5; barriers, removing 38–9; effect of teachers on 24–5
Achievement for All programme 25, 95
action research 115–17
actions, team 70
active learning 13, **57**, 89
A.G. Barr 102
Allan, J. 87–8
andragogy 32, **34**, 36, 44
anti-learning approach, and technology 21
applied learning 9–11, **57**; challenge for 32–4; cycle *12*; defining 11–14; importance of 33–7
aspiration 93–5
assessment, learner 17–19
assessment for learning 18
authentic creative challenge **58**, 113
authentic learning **58**

Bandura, A. 36, 134
behaviourism 36

behaviours: helpless-oriented 94, 96; mastery-oriented 94–6; professional 53–4
beliefs 121–2
Black, P. 18
Bloom, B. 4, 43
Bloom's taxonomy 43
Boy's Wonder Book of Science 22
British Educational Research Association (BERA) 117
Brookfield, S. 120
Bruner, J. 4
Burkey, S. 129

carers *see* parents
case study 5
Castelikns, J. 90
CBI/Pearson report (2016) 10
Center for Curriculum Redesign (US) 11
Centre for Studies on Inclusive Education 86
challenges: for learners 40–1; of learners 92
Chamber of Commerce 72
character 11
Cheminais, R. 38

137

Index

child-centred theories 88
choice, learner 14, 37, 85
classroom groupings 19, 90
Coe, R. 50, 54
cognitive development, effect of
  social interaction on 19, 90
collaboration: with colleagues
  23–4, 102; in teams 66, 70
collaborative learning 19–20, **57**,
  96–7
collaborative reflective learning
  120
colleagues, collaboration with 23–4
communication, in teams 70
competence, in teams 66
compulsory schooling 37
computer literate 22
confidence: of learners 95; of
  teachers 89
connected classroom 20
constructivism *see* social
  constructivism
continual professional
  development (CPD) 52
control of learning 14
Cornwall College Camborne Media
  Department 51
Cornwall Film Festival 51
creative expression 110
creative problem solving 56, **58**
creative teaching 108, 114–17
creative thinking 110
creativity 110–14; creative teacher
  as researcher 114–17;
  importance of 107–10
Criminal Records Bureau (CRB)
  103
critical lenses 120

Deloitte Employability Initiative
  72–5
demonstrations **57**
Design Technology classes 37
Dewey, J. 4
didactic teaching 35, 38

digital technology 21, 22–3, 107–8
disaffection, learner 14, 33
Disclosure and Barring Service
  (DBS) 103
Dweck, C. 94

Earl, L. 70, 89
Eco, U. 109
Education Scotland 78
emotional intelligence, of teachers
  92
employer engagement 62–3, 76–9;
  definition of 62; mentoring
  63–5; motivation in teams 70–1;
  team-working and team-building
  65–7
employment skills 61–2; work-
  related learning on non-
  vocational courses 71–5;
  work-related learning on
  vocational courses 75
engagement of learners 84
England, secondary education in
  35
environment, learning 42, 43,
  50–1, 54, 70, 88; inclusive 19, 90
Esat, K. 86
European Social Fund 113
Everard, K. B. 65, 67, 127
experiential learning 12
extra-curricular activities 95

facilitation of applied learning
  83–4; collaborative learning
  96–7; functional skills 100–2;
  health and safety 103; inclusive
  practice 86–91; mindset of
  learners 94–6; problem-based
  learning 97–100; role of teacher
  84–6; teacher–learner
  relationship 91–5
Fadel, C. 11
feedback 39, 54; in teams 66,
  69–70
Film School 50–1

Index

Fink, D. 70, 89
flipped classroom approach 98–9
formative assessment 17, 96
Foskett, N. 33
Fröbel, F. 4, 88
Fry, S. 22
functional skills (FS) 53, 100–1; teaching 101–2

Gates, B. 99
goals, team 66
Goldacre, B. 114
Golman, D. 92
Google 99

Hall, I. 127
Hargreaves, D. H. 128
Harris Tweed Hebrides 78
health 103
helpless-oriented behaviours 94, 96
Herreid, C. F. 98
Higher Education Academy 62
history of applied learning 4
Hopkins, D. 129
humanism 37

ICE (Innovation, Creativity and Enterprise) House Project 113
inclusive practice 86–91
independent learning 31–2, 38, 43, 52, 84, 92
Independent Safeguarding Authority (ISA) 103
individualised learning see personalised learning
inquiry-based teaching/learning 15–16; assessment 17–19
interaction between teachers and learners 54
Internet 23
inter-personal skills 20, 91

Johns, S. 74–5

Kapp, A. 36
Kettle, J. 62
Khan, S. 98–99
Khan Academy 99
kinaesthetic learning 57
knowledge 11; access, and technology 21
Knowles, M. 36

leaders: and collaboration 23–4; team 66, 67–8, 70
learner-centred education see personalised learning
learning by doing 36, 38
lectures 57
Leitch Report 35
Lenzie Academy 102
lesson 85
literacy skills 101, 109
Local Enterprise Partnership (LEP) 72
Lumby, J. 33

Macmillan Coffee Morning 73
Maslow, A. H. 37, 134
Mason, R. 51
mastery-oriented behaviours 94–6
Mayes, T. 20–1
medical training 2–3
mentoring 63–5, 111–12
metacognition 29, 31–2
meta-learning 11
Microsoft Partners in Learning/ITL Research project 109
mindset, of learners 93, 94–6
Moll, L. C. 89
monitoring, self-evaluation 126–7
Montessori, M. 88
Morris, G. 65, 127
motivation: of learners 89; in teams 70–1

National Progression Award in Harris Tweed 78–9
needs of learners 41–2

139

Index

non-vocational courses, work-related learning on 71–5
Northouse, P. 66
numeracy skills 101, 110

objectives 39, 68, 90, 91, 125, 126
Oldroyd, D. 127
openness, in teams 70
Organisation for Economic Co-operation and Development (OECD) 10–11, 15, 21
ownership: for change 50; of learning 38

parents 53–4; engagement, effect on learners' aspirations 93
Parsons, D. 129
participation barriers, removing 38–9
passion for learning 39
pedagogical heresy 21
pedagogy 32, **34**, 36, 44
peers: reflections of 120; relationships with 19, 90
personalised learning 29, 30–1, 38–9, 40
Personal Learning and Thinking Skills (PLTS) 53
Piaget, J. 36, 88, 135
planning 39, 42, 53, 102, 132
poetry 113
positive attitudes 38, 89
practice: -based approach to self-evaluation 124, *125*; inclusive 86–91; of teachers 48–55
praise 54
praxis-based approach 2, 65
pride, in team 69
prior learning 84, 96
problem-based learning (PBL) 2–3, **58**, 97–100; definition of 3
problem-solving approach 91–2
progression, learner 39; tracking 77
psychology course 56

qualifications-based curricula 4–5
quality teaching 50

REAL (Relevant, Engaging, Active Learning) 50, 55, 63, 64, 131
recognition, in teams 67
reflection-in-action 120
reflection-on-action 120
reflective learning 120–1
ResearchED 114
researcher, creative teacher as 114–17
responsibility: of learners 14, 37, 44, 89, 96; of teachers 5, 36, 50, 52, 86
responsive instruction 90
results-driven structure, of teams 66
reviews, team 69–70
Robinson, K. 10, 98–9, 108
Rogers, C. 14, 30, 37, 134
role models: leaders as 70; teachers as 91
role play 75
Royal Shakespeare Company (RSC) 77

safeguarding 103
safety 103
Sapon-Shevin, M. 86
scaffolding 112
Schiller, N. A. 98
Schön, D. A. 120
Scott, E. 78
self-assessment 73
self-awareness, of teachers 92
self-development 121, 122; skills 31
self-evaluation 121–3; elements of 128; model 124–5, *125*; monitoring 126–7; situations **123**
SEND 93, 95
Senior Leadership Team (SLT) 52

Index

sharing, about learning outcomes 84
Sharples, M. 98
situational leadership, in teams 68
skills 11, 43; for employment 61–2, 71–7; functional 100–2; self-developmental 31; social/inter-personal 20, 91
Skinner, B. 36, 134
social constructivism 36–7
social interaction, effect on cognitive development 19, 90
social skills 20, 91
Stainback, S. 86
Stainback, W. 86
standards of excellence, in teams 66
Stoll, L. 70, 89
stretching, of learners 40–1
student-centred education *see* personalised learning
subject knowledge 50
summative assessment 17
Summerhill School 37
support, for teams 67
Sutton Trust 24
systems, for teachers 24–5

Taleb, N. N. 109
teacher-centred model 36
teacher–learner relationship 89, 90, 91–5; increasing aspiration and access 93–5
teachers 14–15; assessment 17–19; collaborative learning 19–20; development 122; inquiry-based teaching/learning 15–16; interaction with learners 54; role in facilitation of applied learning 84–6; systems for 24–5; technology 20–3

teaching 47–8; practice 48–55; strategies 55, 56, **57**–8
team-building 65–70; Tuckman's stages of 69
team(s): definition of 65–6; effectiveness of 68–70; motivation in 70–1
team-working 65–7
technology 20–3, 107–8
teenagogy 33–7, 44; creating independent learners 43; meeting individual needs of learners 41–2; removing barriers to participation, learning and achievement 38–9; stretching and challenging learners 40–1
Tuckman, B. 68; stages of team building 69

unity, in teams 66

values 121–2; team 68
Visible Media 110–11
vocational courses, work-related learning on 75
Vygotsky, L. S. 19, 36, 90, 135

West-Burnham, J. 68
Whitmore, K. F. 89
William, D. 18
Wilson, D. 126
Wilson, I. 65, 127
work-related learning **58**, 62; health and safety 103; on non-vocational courses 71–5; on vocational courses 75

'Young Leaders in Service' Gold Award 73

Zone of Proximal Development (ZPD) 36

141

Taylor & Francis eBooks

Helping you to choose the right eBooks for your Library

Add Routledge titles to your library's digital collection today. Taylor and Francis ebooks contains over 50,000 titles in the Humanities, Social Sciences, Behavioural Sciences, Built Environment and Law.

Choose from a range of subject packages or create your own!

Benefits for you
» Free MARC records
» COUNTER-compliant usage statistics
» Flexible purchase and pricing options
» All titles DRM-free.

REQUEST YOUR FREE INSTITUTIONAL TRIAL TODAY

Free Trials Available
We offer free trials to qualifying academic, corporate and government customers.

Benefits for your user
» Off-site, anytime access via Athens or referring URL
» Print or copy pages or chapters
» Full content search
» Bookmark, highlight and annotate text
» Access to thousands of pages of quality research at the click of a button.

eCollections – Choose from over 30 subject eCollections, including:

Archaeology	Language Learning
Architecture	Law
Asian Studies	Literature
Business & Management	Media & Communication
Classical Studies	Middle East Studies
Construction	Music
Creative & Media Arts	Philosophy
Criminology & Criminal Justice	Planning
Economics	Politics
Education	Psychology & Mental Health
Energy	Religion
Engineering	Security
English Language & Linguistics	Social Work
Environment & Sustainability	Sociology
Geography	Sport
Health Studies	Theatre & Performance
History	Tourism, Hospitality & Events

For more information, pricing enquiries or to order a free trial, please contact your local sales team: **www.tandfebooks.com/page/sales**

The home of Routledge books

www.tandfebooks.com